Grammar and Writing 8

Student Workbook

First Edition

Christie Curtis

Mary Hake

Houghton Mifflin Harcourt Publishers, Inc.

Grammar and Writing 8

First Edition

Student Workbook

ISBN-13: 978-1-4190-9859-8
ISBN-10:   1-4190-9859-4

Houghton Mifflin Harcourt Publishers, Inc.
181 Ballardvale Street
Wilmington, MA 01887

http://saxonhomeschool.com

Printed in the United States of America.

8 9 10 11 12 13 14 15 16 2266 21 20 19 18

4500697453

Writing 8 Contents

More Practice and Hysterical Fiction

Introduction

The ability to communicate clearly and effectively in writing connects us with people and enhances our prospects for future success in school and in the workplace. We improve our writing skills with practice. Daily journals and informal letters, notes, or emails to friends and family members provide frequent opportunities to use what we have learned in our grammar and writing lessons. In addition, we must practice more formal writing exercises to prepare ourselves for writing assignments that we will receive in high school and college classes.

In *Grammar and Writing 7*, we learned to create all the parts of a complete essay, to write many different types of essays, and to evaluate each type of essay. In addition, we wrote outlines, research papers, imaginative stories, summaries, and poetry. In *Grammar and Writing 8*, we shall practice all these writing forms again, this time with greater depth and skill. You will also learn more about online research—how to find useful web sites and how to evaluate the information.

You are becoming a writer! One of the most important tools you as a writer will need is a small notebook or card file for collecting ideas, for jotting down things that you notice or wonder about, for saving your memories and dreams, and for writing down favorite words, names, and catchy phrases from things you read or hear. You might even keep drawings, photos, or newspaper clippings in your notebook. This is a place to keep bits and pieces that you might someday use in a larger composition—a poem, essay, or story. You will carry this small notebook or card file with you *everywhere* and jot in it often.

In addition to your small notebook or card file, you will need a folder or binder for keeping your daily journals and your writing assignments from this packet. Your three-ring binder will help you to organize your work so that you can easily refer back to earlier assignments when necessary.

Writing
Lessons

LESSON 1

Reviewing the Paragraph

The Paragraph
A **paragraph** is a group of sentences that builds on a main idea, or topic. A good paragraph presents one main idea and develops it with additional sentences giving more specific information about that main idea. The supporting sentences are arranged in a logical order.

The Topic Sentence
The **topic sentence** is a complete sentence telling the main idea of a paragraph. Often the topic sentence is the first sentence of a paragraph, but not always. Topic sentences are underlined in the following paragraphs:

> <u>Elle's favorite place is the Mojave Desert</u>. There at night she gazes at the clear, starry desert sky and identifies each constellation. When the sun comes up, she can see for miles in every direction across the great expanse of uninhabited land. Breathing the fresh air, collecting rocks and minerals, photographing reptiles, and walking desert trails in solitude give Elle much pleasure.

> Walking to school, Jared picked up several pieces of trash and put them into a dumpster. After helping an elderly woman catch her run-away beagle, he lifted a neighbor's newspaper out of a puddle and placed it on dry ground. In the school yard, Jared found an envelope containing five dollars—probably someone's lunch money. This he took to the lost-and-found box in the office. <u>Jared is doing his best to help others and to make his community a cleaner, happier place</u>.

Example 1
The sentences below are all from one paragraph, but they have been mixed up here. Read them all and decide which one is actually the topic sentence. Remember, the topic sentence tells the reader what the whole paragraph is about, not just one part of it. Underline the topic sentence and put the number "1" near it. Next, arrange all of the sentences in a logical order to create one good paragraph.

- Finally, bake the batter in a 350-degree oven for thirty minutes.
- Then pour the batter into a baking dish and spread it evenly.
- 1 You will need a large mixing bowl, a mixing spoon, a baking dish, three ripe bananas, an egg, two cups of flour, a cup of sugar, a teaspoon of baking soda, and one-fourth cup of oil.
- Place all the ingredients in the large bowl and stir them with the spoon until the batter is smooth.
- By following some simple instructions, you can make delicious banana bread.

We sequence the sentences to make this paragraph:

By following some simple instructions, you can make delicious banana bread. You will need a large mixing bowl, a mixing spoon, a baking dish, three ripe bananas, an egg, two cups of flour, a cup of sugar, a teaspoon of baking soda, and one-fourth cup of oil. Place all the ingredients in the large bowl and stir them with the spoon until the batter is smooth. Then pour the batter into a baking dish and spread it evenly. Finally, bake the batter in a 350-degree oven for thirty minutes.

Example 2 Underline the topic sentence in the following paragraph:

Whenever Debby encounters a stray dog or cat, she tries to find it a home. She has nursed hundreds of sick or injured creatures back to health. Debby loves animals. She has eighty-two cats, eleven dogs, six chickens, and two horses. Many people call on her for advice about caring for their pets.

We see that the paragraph above is all about how Debby loves animals. Therefore, we underline the topic sentence as follows:

Whenever Debby encounters a stray dog or cat, she tries to find it a home. She has nursed hundreds of sick or injured creatures back to health. **Debby loves animals.** She has eighty-two cats, eleven dogs, six chickens, and two horses. Many people call on her for advice about caring for their pets.

Practice Arrange the sentences below in a logical order to create a good paragraph. Write the paragraph on the lines provided. Then underline the topic sentence.

- After the heavy rain ceased, Mrs. Perez picked up her lost dog and handed Manny a freshly-baked loaf of bread to thank him.

- Then he notified the owner, a Mrs. Perez, and gave her his address.

- During a thunderstorm, Manny found a wet, shivering cocker spaniel on his porch.

- First Manny checked the dog's license and found the owner's phone number.

_____

_____

_____

_____

_____

_____

_____

_____

_____

_____

_____

_____

_____

_____

Additional Practice   Underline the topic sentence in each paragraph below.

a.   While she sleeps, Margaret dreams about chess tournaments. Upon waking she begins thinking about how she can convince her friends to play games of chess with her. Throughout the day, she ponders new strategies for winning the game. There is nothing she would rather do than play chess. Margaret is a chess enthusiast.

_____

b.   Opossums are a benefit to any area they inhabit. They eat cockroaches and garden pests such as slugs and snails. They also eat the overripe fruit that litters the ground. Resistant to disease, these friendly creatures seldom carry rabies. Constantly grooming themselves, they are almost always clean. Best of all, they are not aggressive and will not attack humans.

_____

c.   Quan has been studying geology, botany, and zoology. He reads every book he can find on these subjects, and he watches many nature documentaries on television. Quan is preparing to become a forest ranger. Whenever he has an opportunity, he goes hiking and camping in the wilderness, where he feels at home, and where he can identify every plant, animal, and insect he sees.

Each of the following paragraphs contains a sentence that does not support the topic sentence. Read the paragraphs carefully. Then draw a line through the sentence that does not belong in each paragraph.

d.   Melissa wanted to write a report on her favorite music composer. First she searched her uncle's vast book cases but found nothing about this composer. She didn't find any helpful books on the shelves of the school library either. Washing dishes is more fun than doing homework. Even the large municipal library had no books about a composer named Hieden. When the search engine on her computer also produced nothing, Melissa felt like screaming with frustration. Finally, her teacher pointed out that she had misspelled the composer's name, which is Haydn instead of Hieden.

e.   I am running out of patience with my bicycle tires. They were flat yesterday morning, so I had to pump them, which made me late for school. Later, I spent all my allowance on new bicycle tires. Besides that, I flunked my spelling test. And now, after riding along the horse trail for less than a mile, I have found more than a dozen puncture weeds in each of my new tires. Surely they cannot hold air; they are full of holes! What am I going to do?

Practice writing a paragraph for each of the following topic sentences. Add at least three sentences to support and/or more fully explain the topic sentence.

1.   We can encourage one another during hard times.

2.   Fall is an enjoyable time of the year.

3.   Caring for a pet requires responsibility.

Hint: Your sentences following the topic sentence might answer some of the *who, what, when, where, why,* and *how* questions below.

1.   *Why* should we encourage one another during hard times?
     When do people need encouragement?
     How can we encourage one another?

2.   *What* makes fall an enjoyable time of the year?
     Where do you enjoy the fall?
     Who enjoys the fall?

3.   *Why* does caring for a pet require responsibility?
     What kind of care does a pet require?
     How can one demonstrate responsibility in caring for a pet?

LESSON 2

Reviewing the Parts of a Complete Essay

Our goal is to write clear, coherent, focused essays. To accomplish this, we must keep in mind the structure of a complete essay. In this lesson, we shall briefly review the **parts of a complete essay.**

Complete Essay

A **complete essay** is constructed of three main parts:

1. Introductory Paragraph

2. Body or Support Paragraphs

3. Concluding Paragraph

Now let us recall all that is included in these three main parts of an essay.

(1) Introductory Paragraph

The **introductory paragraph,** the first paragraph of an essay, introduces the general theme or subject of the essay. To do this, and to attract the reader's interest, the introductory paragraph contains a very clear sentence that tells exactly what the entire essay will be about. That one, very clear sentence comes near the beginning of the introductory paragraph and is called the *thesis statement.* For this reason, the introductory paragraph is often called the *thesis paragraph.*

Thesis Statement

Every essay that we write is an attempt to persuade, influence, or explain something. That something is our **thesis statement,** and it is always in the introductory (first) paragraph. The thesis statement not only tells the reader exactly what the essay is about but also clearly states your position on the topic. There should be no doubt in a reader's mind exactly what you are writing about and exactly what your position is after reading your thesis statement.

We do not use the words, "I think" or "I feel" in our thesis statement. There are two reasons for this. First, it is obvious that this is your opinion, so it is redundant to say, "I think." Second, when you use "I feel" or "I think," it sounds as though you really do not believe strongly in what you are writing.

Write with confidence! Write with a sense of purpose! Do not be wishy-washy. Write as though you know exactly what you are talking about, and state it firmly.

THESIS STATEMENT: *Procrastination is a destructive habit for three reasons.*

THESIS STATEMENT: *More time in the classroom does not necessarily result in more student learning.*

Introductory Sentence

The first sentence of an essay, the **introductory sentence,** should grab the reader's interest. This sentence can be long or short. It can be opinion or fact. It can even be more than one sentence. It is an introduction to the thesis statement, and it should make the reader want to know more about the subject of the essay.

We usually do not begin with a question as the introductory sentence. A question often makes a weak introduction. The first thing that pops into a reader's mind when he or she reads, "Have you ever wondered," or "What if," is "No," and then your essay is over. The reader is not going to read on. For example, consider what might happen if an essay began, "Do you think the school year should be lengthened by a month?" The reader might very well think, "No," and stop reading.

INTRODUCTORY SENTENCES: *There are laws against drug abuse because it ruins people's lives. And there are laws against drinking and driving because it is dangerous. But some human behaviors are not against the law even though they are harmful. Procrastination is a prime example.*

INTRODUCTORY SENTENCE: *Many parents believe their children's school days should be longer, yet others disagree.*

(2) Body Paragraphs

Body paragraphs, or support paragraphs, come after the introductory (first) paragraph and before the final paragraph. Body paragraphs provide the evidence to prove your thesis statement, and they provide the information through examples or facts that helps the reader understand exactly what you, the writer, want to communicate.

Topic Sentence

Each body paragraph must have a **topic sentence.** A topic sentence is a complete sentence, usually at the beginning of a body paragraph. It tells the reader exactly what the paragraph is about and is followed by supporting sentences.

Supporting Sentences: **Supporting sentences** support, prove, or explain the topic sentence of that paragraph. At least three supporting sentences are usually needed to make a strong paragraph.

Experience, fact, or example sentences are always the strongest arguments to prove a point, so they should immediately follow the topic sentence to build a strong paragraph. An **experience or example sentence** explains or illustrates an event that helps to prove, support or explain your topic sentence.

> EXPERIENCE SENTENCES: *Last summer I camped in the wilderness and studied desert plants and animals. I collected rock specimens, photographed creatures, and read several books on wildlife, rocks, and minerals. I learned more than I would have by sitting in a classroom.*

> EXAMPLE SENTENCE: *For example, if you put off doing your work today, you'll have more, maybe even too much, work to do tomorrow.*

A **fact sentence** displays a fact from research that supports or proves your topic sentence.

> FACT SENTENCE: *Dr. Fussbudget's recent survey concludes that people who habitually procrastinate are fifty percent more prone to anxiety and stress than those who do not procrastinate.*

A fact is a piece of information that can be proven to be true. On the other hand, opinion is something that cannot be proven true or false. For example, it is a fact that Alaska is the largest state in the Union. It is opinion to say that Alaska is the most beautiful state in the Union.

Your opinions are your thoughts or feelings about a particular subject. **Opinion sentences,** communicating thoughts and feelings that are directly related to the topic sentence, may follow experience and fact sentences to further develop the body paragraph.

> OPINION SENTENCES: *The desert is a wonderful place for learning. It is an explorer's paradise. One can study while enjoying the quiet and the scenery.*

> OPINION SENTENCE: *History is more difficult than math, so you should do your history homework first, before you become too tired to think.*

Other kinds of support sentences, which we shall discuss in a later lesson, include definitions, anecdotes, arguments, and analogies.

Transitions You will usually have three or more body paragraphs in your essay, plus a concluding paragraph. You should place those paragraphs in the most logical order, with, of course, the concluding paragraph appearing last.

However, even though each body paragraph is a separate idea supporting the thesis statement, a good writer can make those separate ideas flow smoothly from one into another into another through the use of transitions.

A **transition** is a word, phrase, or clause that links one subject or idea to another. A transition is placed at the beginning of a body paragraph to help the essay "flow" from one paragraph to another. Effective transitions make the ideas easier for the reader to follow.

Typical transitions include the following:

Another thing…	Likewise…
The second reason…	Similarly…
Furthermore…	In the same way…
As a result…	Consequently…
However…	On the other hand…
Therefore…	In conclusion…

(3) Concluding Paragraph The final paragraph of an essay, the **concluding paragraph,** should both summarize and reinforce the ideas and opinions expressed in the body of the essay. The concluding paragraph includes two important parts:

1. a restatement of the thesis statement

2. a reference to each of the topic sentences

Good writers know that "last words" leave a lasting impression.

As you work through this writing packet, you will frequently refer to the "parts of a complete essay" that are described in this lesson. Keep these and all other writing pages in your folder or binder where you can easily find them.

Now, carefully review the sample essay on the next page.

Example   Here is an example of a five-paragraph essay that contains all the essential parts:

introductory sentence

Introductory Paragraph

Learning to write well is one of the most important skills we need to master. *The ability to communicate clearly and effectively in writing connects us with people and enhances our prospects for future success in school and in the workplace.*

thesis statement (italics)

In the first place, writing well allows us to communicate with other people. We can share our thoughts and feelings with others by writing personal letters, business letters, notes, and emails. Often, people's friendships or business relationships are dependent on their ability to keep in touch with people by way of written correspondence.

Body Paragraphs

Secondly, our success in school both now and in the future depends on our ability to write well. Teachers may require us to be able to express on paper what we have learned in classes such as social studies, English, and science. We will also need to be able to write effectively on college applications.

In addition, we shall use our writing skills in our future workplace. A well-written job application might help us to acquire the job we desire. Moreover, most jobs and professions entail writing. Teachers, doctors, pastors, secretaries, mechanics, and business people all have to write daily in their workplaces.

Concluding Paragraph

In conclusion, the ability to write skillfully will help us in our relationships with people, in our schooling, and in our future workplace. No skill is more important to our success than writing.

restatement of thesis with reference to each topic sentence

In the essay above, transitions are circled and topic sentences are underlined.

Practice   Refer to the sample five-paragraph essay above to complete 1–5 on the blank lines provided.

1. Write the thesis statement of the essay.

_____

2. Write the introductory sentence of the essay.

_____

3. Write the topic sentence for the first body paragraph.

_____

4. Write the word group used as a transition for the first body paragraph of the essay. _____

5. Write the words used as a transition to the concluding paragraph. _____

A Memory Tool The chart below helps us remember the essential parts of a complete, five-paragraph essay.

ESSAY PLAN

Introductory Paragraph	Introductory sentence(s) Thesis statement
Body or Support Paragraph	*Topic sentence* Support sentences: experience, fact, example, opinion, or other
Body or Support Paragraph	*Topic sentence* Support sentences: experience, fact, example, opinion, or other
Body or Support Paragraph	*Topic sentence* Support sentences: experience, fact, example, opinion, or other
Concluding Paragraph	Restatement of the thesis Reference to each topic sentence

---

Practice In the chart below, replace each blank to complete the essential parts of a complete, five-paragraph essay.

ESSAY PLAN

Introductory Paragraph	_____ sentence(s) _____ statement
Body or Support Paragraph	_____ *sentence* _____ sentences: experience, fact, example, opinion, or other
Body or Support Paragraph	*Topic sentence* Support sentences: _____, fact, example, opinion, or other
Body or Support Paragraph	*Topic sentence* Support sentences: experience, _____, _____, opinion, or other
Concluding Paragraph	Restatement of the _____ Reference to each _____ sentence

On the page that follows, you will find a memory tool to help you memorize this chart.

Example Study the chart from the previous page. Then try to reproduce it from memory on a separate piece of paper.

We simply use this chart as a memory tool to help us keep in mind the structure of a complete essay. We may abbreviate in order to reproduce it quickly.

Essay Plan	
Intro. Para.	Intro. sent. Thesis statement
Body Para.	Top. sent. Sup. sents.: exp., fact, ex., op., or other
B. P.	T. S. S. S.: exp., fact, ex., op., or other
B. P.	T. S. S. S.: exp., fact, ex., op., or other
Concl. Para.	Restatement of thesis Ref. to each T. S.

Practice Study the chart showing the parts of a five-paragraph essay. Then reproduce it from memory, abbreviating if you wish. After checking your reproduction of the chart to be sure it contains all the essential parts, place this assignment in your folder or binder for quick reference in the future.

Preparing to Write a Complete Essay

The Thesis Statement   Keeping in mind the structure of a complete essay described in Lesson 2, we will prepare to write a five-paragraph essay with the following thesis statement:

Pets can be expensive.

Brainstorming   Brainstorming is a method of quickly capturing ideas about a topic or problem. One way to brainstorm is illustrated below.

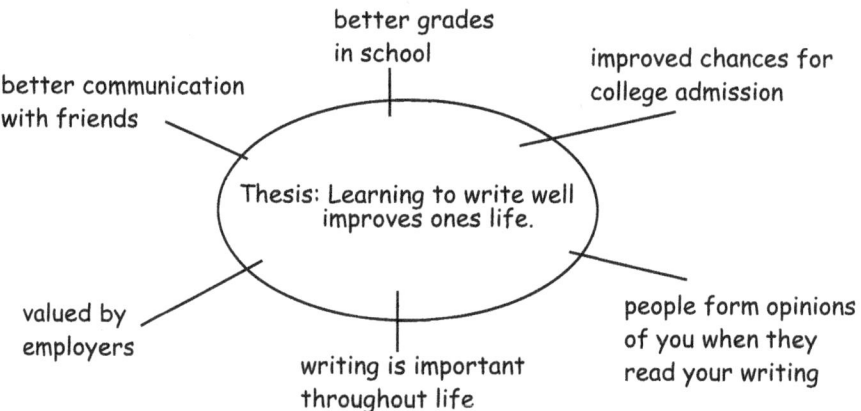

For the next few minutes, use this model to record brainstorming ideas for the thesis statement "Pets can be expensive." You may use the worksheet on the following page. Quickly begin to write in the area outside the circle any and all words that come into your mind as soon as they come into your mind.

- Write quickly. Do not allow your pencil to stop moving.

- Do not worry about spelling or neatness.

- Do not worry about the word order or location.

- Don't think, just write.

Write for about three minutes or until your paper is covered with words, whichever comes first.

When you have finished, you will almost certainly have several ideas to help you get started writing your essay.

Brainstorming for Body Paragraph Ideas

Pets can be expensive.

Organizing your Ideas

After you have brainstormed, the next step is to look at the ideas you have generated and identify the ones that best support your thesis statement. Follow these steps to organize your ideas:

1. Take a moment to look at the words or groups of words you wrote. Some of them will begin to stand out as relating very well to the thesis, and others will begin to look as though they don't belong or are not as strong.

2. Choose at least three different words or groups of words that best support the thesis. Circle them. If you cannot decide on just three, you may circle four or five. If you circle more than three words or groups of words, you have more than enough support for your thesis statement. You can write several body paragraphs of support, or you might later decide to combine one or more arguments or to eliminate the weaker ones.

3. These circled word groups will become your *body paragraph ideas*. Write these ideas on the lines provided below (or type them into your computer file), leaving space underneath each idea to add more notes later for expanding the paragraphs.

4. Look at your *body paragraph ideas* and try to determine the order in which they should be arranged in the body of your essay to best support your thesis. Number the ideas. You can rearrange the order or even eliminate or add additional body paragraphs at any time as ideas come to you.

| # | | *Body paragraph idea:* _____

_____

_____

_____

_____

| # | | *Body paragraph idea:* _____

_____

_____

_____

_____

| # | | *Body paragraph idea:* _____ |

_____

_____

_____

| # | | *Body paragraph idea:* _____ |

_____

_____

_____

_____

Forming Topic Sentences Once you have selected the best ideas from your brainstorming and written them on the lines above, the next step is to take those ideas and form them into topic sentences. Each topic sentence will become a main idea for your essay's body paragraphs.

Practice Write at least three topic sentences that clearly support your thesis statement. Keep this assignment in your folder or binder. In Lesson 4, we shall expand these topic sentences into body paragraphs and then complete an essay.

Topic sentence: _____

_____

_____

Topic sentence: _____

_____

_____

Topic sentence: _____

_____

_____

Topic sentence: _____

_____

_____

Writing a Complete Essay

In Lesson 3, you brainstormed and created ideas to support the thesis statement "Pets can be expensive." You also chose the best of those ideas and put them in the order that best supports the thesis statement. Then you used the ideas to create topic sentences. Now you are ready to write the complete essay. If necessary, refer to Lesson 2 for a description of each part of the essay.

Practice Using the topic sentences you wrote for Lesson 3, follow the steps below to complete the essay.

1. For each topic sentence, write a body paragraph to support the thesis statement. To expand your paragraph, you might add experience sentences, opinion sentences, example sentences, or fact sentences.

2. Create an introductory paragraph with an introductory sentence that will grab the reader's interest, and a sentence that states the thesis.

3. Write a concluding paragraph that includes a restatement of the thesis and a reference to each of the topic sentences.

4. Add transitions between body paragraphs to make your ideas easier for the reader to follow. Pay special attention to the transition into the concluding paragraph.

5. Finally, put all the parts together to form a complete essay. As you are working, make any necessary corrections to your previous work. You might add or subtract words, or make any other change that results in a more effective essay. Keep this essay in your folder or binder. You will evaluate it in the next lesson.

Evaluating Your Essay

The Writing Process

All of the writing we do should be viewed as "work in progress." Even after you have turned in an essay to your teacher for a grade, you should not feel it can never be touched again. The knowledge that *writing is a process* should guide your thinking throughout the construction of an essay. From the first steps in organizing your thoughts, to creating body paragraphs, to adding transitions, you should feel free to make changes to improve your work.

At each step of the writing process, you should stop to reevaluate both your thoughts and the words you have placed on the page.

It is helpful to do this after each step of the writing process. It is also important to do this after the entire essay is written. In fact, it is probably most helpful to complete an essay, then walk away from it for a day or two, and then come back and read it again.

Many times, sentences that seemed good the first time appear much different a day or two later. Furthermore, you may find that more ideas have come to you, or ideas that were somewhat muddled before have become clearer. Two days later, you can write them in a way that is more meaningful to the reader.

Use the following guidelines to help you evaluate your writing.

Evaluating Your Writing

Do not be afraid to change what you have already written. Just because it was typed or written on paper in ink does not mean it cannot be improved.

Ask yourself these questions throughout the writing process:

- Is my introductory sentence interesting? *If it is not interesting to you, it certainly will not be interesting to the reader.*

- Do I have a thesis statement that clearly explains the subject of this essay? (For this assignment, the thesis was given to you.)

- Does my thesis statement clearly state my position?

- Does each body paragraph have a clear topic sentence at the beginning that tells the reader exactly what the paragraph will be about? *Read each topic sentence without the rest of the paragraph to see if it can stand alone as a strong idea.*

- Are there other personal experiences or factual examples that I can add to help improve my credibility and help the reader to better understand my point?

- In my opinion sentences have I described my emotions and feelings so well that they create a picture in the mind of the reader to help him or her feel the same as I feel?

- Does each paragraph (except for the first) begin with an effective transition?

- Are there other arguments that I can add as additional body paragraphs to help me prove my point?

- Are some of my arguments weak and unconvincing? Should they be removed because they do not help me prove my point?

- Do my body paragraphs appear in the best possible order to prove my point? Could I place them in a different order that is more logical or effective?

- Is each sentence constructed as well as it should be? *Read each sentence in each paragraph as if it were the only sentence on the page. This helps you to catch sentence fragments, run-on sentences, misspellings, and grammatical errors. If you are working on a computer, put blank lines between each sentence, so you actually see only one full sentence at a time on your screen. This will make sentence fragments jump out at you.*

- Does my concluding paragraph summarize and reinforce the ideas and opinions expressed in the essay?

Practice Use the Evaluation Form on the following page to evaluate the essay you wrote for Lesson 4. Read your essay carefully as you check for the items listed on the Evaluation Form. Write YES or NO in the blank next to each question.

When you are finished, you will either be confident that you have a strong essay, or you will know where it needs to be improved.

If you answered NO to one or more of the questions on the Evaluation Form, rewrite to improve those areas.

When you can answer YES to every question on the Evaluation Form, you will have completed this assignment.

Essay Evaluation Form

Thesis: _____

_____ Is my introductory sentence interesting? *If it is not interesting to you, it certainly won't be interesting to the reader.*

_____ Do I have a thesis statement that clearly explains the subject of this essay?

_____ Does my thesis statement clearly state my position?

_____ Does each body paragraph have a clear topic sentence at the beginning that tells the reader exactly what the paragraph will be about? *Read each topic sentence without the rest of the paragraph to see if it can stand alone as a strong idea.*

_____ Have I included personal experiences that improve my credibility and help the reader to better understand my point?

_____ In my opinion sentences have I described my emotions and feelings so well that they create a picture in the mind of the reader to help him or her feel the same as I feel?

_____ Does each paragraph (except for the first paragraph) begin with an effective transition?

_____ Have I included every strong argument to prove my point?

_____ Are all of my arguments strong and convincing? Do they all help to prove my point?

_____ Do my body paragraphs appear in the best possible order to prove my point? Is their order logical and effective?

_____ Is each sentence structured as well as it could be? *Read each sentence in each paragraph as if it were the only sentence on the page. This helps you catch fragments and run-on sentences and evaluate the overall strength or weakness of each sentence.*

_____ Does my concluding paragraph summarize and reinforce the ideas and opinions expressed in the essay?

Supporting a Topic Sentence with Definitions, Anecdotes, Arguments, and Analogies

We have learned that a topic sentence states the main idea of a paragraph and that the remainder of the paragraph's sentences should clearly and completely prove that the topic sentence is true.

We have practiced developing a body paragraph by adding the most common supporting sentences—experience, example, fact, and opinion sentences—to go along with the topic sentence.

In this lesson, we shall discuss other ways to develop a paragraph by adding detailed information that relates to the topic sentence. We can support a topic sentence by adding definitions, anecdotes, arguments, and analogies. These methods of building paragraphs will be useful when we write other types of essays in later lessons.

Notice how we use these different methods to support the following topic sentence:

Procrastination may cause consternation.

Definitions   To explain the topic sentence, we can define a term or a concept. **Definitions** may help the reader to understand more fully the meaning of the topic sentence.

> Procrastination may cause consternation. *To procrastinate is to put off doing something until a future time; to delay. Consternation is dismay leading to confusion, disappointment, or fear.*

Anecdotes   To entertain the reader while illustrating our point, we can write an **anecdote,** a short account of an incident, something that happened to us or to someone we know, which relates to the topic sentence.

> Procrastination may cause consternation. *Clyde intended to see a magnificent Broadway show last spring, but he didn't buy his ticket right away. He procrastinated. When Clyde went to purchase his ticket, they were sold out. What a disappointment!*

Arguments In some kinds of writing, especially in persuasive writing, logical **arguments** can help to support our topic sentence. An argument might seek to disprove an opposing viewpoint.

> Procrastination may cause consternation. *Some people argue that procrastination is a virtue, a necessary component of a relaxed lifestyle. However, the consequences of procrastinating usually add more stress, not less, to one's life.*

Analogies Sometimes we can use an **analogy** to clarify a point. An analogy is a comparison. To be effective, the two things being compared must have many similarities. Usually interesting to a reader, an analogy will help the reader to better understand the topic sentence.

> Procrastination may cause consternation. *A procrastinator is as powerless and ineffective as an automobile without an engine.*

Practice For a–d, use the following topic sentence: *We can each do our part to preserve our natural resources.*

a. Write a *definition* that could be used to expand the topic sentence above.

_____

_____

_____

_____

b. Write an *anecdote* to illustrate the topic sentence.

_____

_____

_____

_____

c. Write an *argument* that might prove the topic sentence.

_____

_____

_____

_____

d. Write an *analogy*, or comparison, to clarify the topic sentence.

_____

_____

_____

_____

Additional Practice Using the methods that you have learned in this lesson, expand each of the following topic sentences into a paragraph of at least five sentences.

1. When we are old enough, it is our civic duty to vote in local, state, and national elections.

2. United States citizens should know how their government works.

3. A good leader has integrity.

4. The President of the United States has a difficult job.

5. Learning a foreign language can help you make new friends.

Preparing to Write a Persuasive Essay

Four Purposes for Writing
Every piece of writing has a purpose. There are four basic purposes for writing: narrative, expository, descriptive, and persuasive.

Narrative writing tells a story or relates a series of events. A composition describing your six-day tour of battlefields in New England would be narrative writing. In Lesson 20, you will write a narrative essay telling about a personal experience of your choice.

Expository writing gives information or explains. A scientific article entitled "How a Seismograph Records Earth Vibrations" would be an example of expository writing. Another example was your essay explaining how procrastination can cause consternation.

Descriptive writing describes a person, place, or thing. Examples include a brochure describing the beautiful Crater Lake in Oregon, a personal composition about your best friend, and a "Lost Kitten" poster that tells exactly what the lost kitten looks like. In Lessons 22 and 23, you will practice this type of writing by describing a person whom you can observe.

Persuasive writing attempts to convince someone to do or believe something. An advertisement for Hooey's Pet Shampoo, an article about the importance of preserving a wild duck habitat, and a campaign flyer urging voters to elect a certain candidate are all examples of persuasive writing. In this lesson, you will write a persuasive essay.

The Persuasive Essay
Keeping in mind the structure of a complete essay described in Lesson 2, we shall prepare to write a persuasive essay using the following sentence as our thesis statement:

Eighth-grade students should be required to pass a United States Constitution exam before graduating to the next grade level.

The goal of this essay will be to convince or *persuade* the reader that eighth-grade students should be required to pass a United States Constitution exam before graduating.

Persuasive essays usually deal with controversial topics, subjects that have two sides. If you prefer, you may argue the opposite side and rewrite the thesis statement to read, "Eighth-grade students *should not* be required to pass a United States Constitution exam before graduating to the next grade level."

As you do your brainstorming for this exercise, you will find out if there are enough strong arguments to support your thesis. This is why brainstorming before you write is such an important exercise. It saves you a great deal of time by convincing you that your thesis statement can or cannot be supported as well as giving you the main ideas for all of your topic sentences.

Your essay will prove that your thesis statement is correct. You will use several arguments to convince the reader of this.

Brainstorming

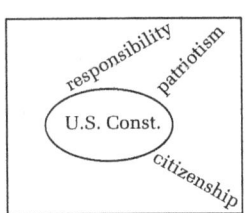

Brainstorming is always our first step in writing an essay. Recall from Writing Lesson 3 that we draw a circle in the middle of a blank sheet of paper. Inside the circle, write the thesis statement. Then quickly begin to write in the area outside the circle any and all words that come into your mind as soon as they come into your mind.

- Write quickly, and do not worry about spelling or neatness.

- Write for about three minutes or until your paper is covered with words, whichever comes first.

- As you write, continue to read your thesis statement in the middle of the circle. This will keep you focused.

Organizing your Ideas

After you have brainstormed, look at the ideas you have generated and identify the ones that best support your thesis statement. Follow these steps to organize your ideas:

1. Take a moment to look at the words or groups of words you wrote. Some of them will begin to stand out as relating very well to the thesis; they will firmly argue your point and convince the reader. Others will begin to look as though they don't belong or are not as strong.

2. Choose at least three different words or groups of words that best support the thesis. Circle them. If you cannot decide on just three, you may circle four or five. If you

circle more than three words or groups of words, you have more than enough support for your thesis statement. You can write several body paragraphs of support, or you might later decide to combine one or more arguments or to eliminate the weaker ones.

3. These circled word groups will become your *body paragraph ideas*. Write these ideas on a separate piece of paper leaving space underneath each idea to add more notes later for expanding the paragraphs.

4. Look at your body paragraph ideas and try to determine the order in which they should be arranged in the body of your essay to best support your thesis. Number the ideas. You can rearrange the order or even eliminate or add additional body paragraphs at any time as ideas come to you.

Forming Topic Sentences Once you have selected the best ideas from your brainstorming and placed them on a separate page, take those ideas and form them into topic sentences. Each topic sentence will become a main idea for your essay's body paragraphs.

Practice Write at least three topic sentences that clearly support your thesis statement. In Lesson 8, we shall develop these topic sentences into body paragraphs and then complete the persuasive essay.

Topic sentence: _____

_____

_____

Topic sentence: _____

_____

_____

Topic sentence: _____

_____

_____

Topic sentence: _____

_____

_____

LESSON 8

Writing a Persuasive Essay

In Lesson 7, you prepared to write your persuasive essay. By brainstorming, you gathered ideas. You chose the best of those ideas and put them in the order that best supports your thesis statement. Then you used the ideas to create at least three topic sentences. Now you are ready to write the complete essay. If necessary, refer to Lesson 2 for a review of all the parts of an essay.

Practice Using the topic sentences you wrote for Lesson 7, follow the steps below to complete the persuasive essay.

1. For each topic sentence, write a body paragraph to support the thesis statement. Refer back to Lesson 6 for different ways to expand a topic sentence into a paragraph. In addition to experience and opinion sentences, you might write definitions, examples, facts, anecdotes, arguments, or analogies that support the topic sentence.

2. Create an introductory paragraph and a concluding paragraph. Remember that the introductory sentence should grab the reader's interest and that the "last words" of your conclusion will leave a lasting impression.

3. Add transitions between body paragraphs to make your ideas easier for the reader to follow. Pay special attention to the transition into the concluding paragraph.

4. Finally, put all the parts together to form a complete essay. As you are working, make any necessary corrections to your previous work. You might add things, take things out, or make any other change that results in a more convincing, persuasive essay.

Additional Practice (Optional) After you have evaluated your persuasive essay using the guidelines in Lesson 9, you might try writing another persuasive essay on one of the topics listed below. Choose "should" or "should not" to complete your thesis statement.

1. School cafeterias (should, should not) stop selling soda to students.

2. High school students (should, should not) be allowed to smoke on the campus of public high schools.

3. Dogs and other pets (should, should not) be allowed on public beaches.

4. Fourteen-year-olds (should, should not) be allowed to vote in general elections.

5. People (should, should not) have to pay a fee to visit a national park.

6. My school day (should, should not) be shortened by one hour.

7. Property owners (should, should not) be compelled to rid their property of any birds or animals that cause trouble.

8. Bears (should, should not) be allowed to roam free in areas where people live.

9. High school students (should, should not) be allowed to wear whatever they want to school.

10. Fourteen-year-olds (should, should not) be allowed to drive.

www.saxonhomeschool.com
©Houghton Mifflin Harcourt Publishers, Inc.

Grammar and Writing 8
Student Workbook, 9781419098598

Evaluating the Persuasive Essay

We have learned that all of the writing we do is "work in progress." The knowledge that *writing is a process* guides our thinking throughout the construction of an essay. From the first steps in organizing our thoughts, to creating body paragraphs, to adding transitions, we constantly make changes to improve our work.

At each step of the writing process, we should stop to reevaluate both our thoughts and the words we have placed on the page.

Evaluating Your Writing
In Lesson 8, you completed your persuasive essay. Now that some time has passed, you are ready to evaluate it using the following guidelines.

Ask yourself these questions:

- Is my introductory sentence interesting? *If it is not interesting to you, it certainly will not be interesting to the reader.*

- Does my thesis statement clearly state my position?

- Does each body paragraph have a clear topic sentence at the beginning that tells the reader exactly what the paragraph will be about? *Read each topic sentence without the rest of the paragraph to see if it can stand alone as a strong idea.*

- Does each of my topic sentences strongly support my thesis statement?

- Are there other personal experiences, facts, examples, arguments, anecdotes, or analogies, that I can add to help improve my credibility and help the reader to better understand my point?

- In my opinion sentences have I described my emotions and feelings so well that they create a picture in the mind of the reader that helps him or her feel the same as I feel?

- Does each paragraph (except for the first) begin with an effective transition?

- Are there other arguments that I can add as additional body paragraphs to help me prove my point?

- Are some of my arguments weak and unconvincing? Should they be removed because they do not help me prove my point?

- Do my body paragraphs appear in the best possible order to prove my point? Could I place them in a different order that is more logical or effective?

- Is each sentence constructed as well as it should be? *Read each sentence in each paragraph as if it were the only sentence on the page. This helps you to find and correct sentence fragments, run-on sentences, misspellings, and grammatical errors.*

- Does my concluding paragraph summarize and reinforce the ideas and opinions expressed in the essay? Have I convinced the reader that my thesis statement is true?

Practice Use the Evaluation Form on the page following this lesson to evaluate the persuasive essay you wrote for Lesson 8. Read your essay carefully as you check for the items listed on the Evaluation Form. Write YES or NO in the blank next to each question.

When you are finished, you will either be confident that you have a strong essay, or you will know where it needs to be improved.

If you answered NO to one or more of the questions on the Evaluation Form, rewrite to improve those areas.

When you can answer YES to every question on the Evaluation Form, you will have completed this assignment.

Persuasive Essay Evaluation Form

Thesis: _____

_____ Is my introductory sentence interesting? *If it is not interesting to you, it certainly won't be interesting to the reader.*

_____ Do I have a thesis statement that clearly explains the subject of this essay?

_____ Does my thesis statement clearly state my position?

_____ Does each body paragraph have a clear topic sentence at the beginning that tells the reader exactly what the paragraph will be about? *Read each topic sentence without the rest of the paragraph to see if it can stand alone as a strong idea.*

_____ Are there any other experiences, facts, or examples that I can add to help improve my credibility and help the reader to better understand my point?

_____ In my opinion sentences have I described my emotions and feelings so well that they create a picture in the mind of the reader to help him or her feel the same as I feel?

_____ Does each paragraph (except for the first paragraph) begin with an effective transition?

_____ Have I included every strong argument to prove my point?

_____ Are all of my arguments strong and convincing?

_____ Do my body paragraphs appear in the best possible order to prove my point?

_____ Is each sentence structured as well as it could be? *Read each sentence in each paragraph as if it were the only sentence on the page. This helps you catch fragments and run-on sentences and evaluate the overall strength or weakness of each sentence.*

_____ Does my concluding paragraph summarize and reinforce the ideas and opinions expressed in the essay?

Writing a Strong Thesis Statement

The thesis statement clearly tells what the entire essay is about. We have practiced writing a complete essay based on an assigned thesis statement. In this lesson, we shall practice creating our own thesis statements for assigned topics.

We remember that the thesis statement not only tells the reader exactly what the essay is about but also clearly states the writer's position on the topic.

Brainstorming When faced with an assigned topic, we prepare by brainstorming in order to generate ideas and thoughts.

The first step in brainstorming is choosing your direction. You would not get into a car and just begin to drive, expecting to arrive at nowhere in particular. You need to know where you are going before you pull out of the driveway. In other words, you must think about the topic, choose your direction or focus, and prepare to define what your essay is about.

For example, if the assignment is to write about the qualities that make a good President of the United States, your thesis statement could begin, "The qualities that make a good President are …"

After brainstorming about the topic, perhaps you have decided that there are four specific qualities that make a good President. If so, your thesis statement might be the following:

> *There are four important qualities that make a good President.*

Practice Below are ten topics that could be given to you as subjects for essays. For each topic, brainstorm briefly. Then write a declarative sentence that could be used as a strong thesis statement for a complete essay.

1. The best things about our country

_____

_____

2. The qualities that make a true friend

_____

_____

3. Why a person should learn mathematics

_____

_____

4. Things that you would like to change about yourself if you could

_____

_____

5. What you will do differently as a student this year from what you did last year

_____

_____

6. Some ways that you can help others

_____

_____

7. Some events you'll always remember

_____

_____

8. What you can do to improve or maintain your physical health

_____

_____

9. Your ideas for improving education in our country

_____

_____

10. Kinds of things that give you a long-lasting sense of joy

_____

_____

Preparing to Write an Expository Essay

The purpose of expository writing is to inform or explain. Expository writing tells why or how. The following might be titles for expository essays:

"How to Harvest Macadamia Nuts"

"New Smoke Alarm Technology"

"Where to Purchase the Best Produce"

"Why the Field Mouse Makes a Good Pet"

"Building a Tree House from Bamboo"

A good expository essay is well organized and clear. It might offer an explanation of how something works, information about a specific subject, or instructions for doing something.

In this lesson, we shall prepare to write an expository essay that explains how to paint the exterior of a house.

Our goal is to write easy-to-follow instructions, which will require a detailed description of the process. Therefore, we shall break down the actions and carefully sequence them in a logical or practical order so that the reader can understand our step-by-step method of painting the exterior of a house.

Brainstorming In order to generate thoughts and ideas, we shall brainstorm before creating a thesis statement for our *how-to* essay.

- Write quickly, and do not worry about spelling or neatness.

- Write for about three minutes or until your paper is covered with words, whichever comes first.

Writing a Thesis Statement Now it is time to state the purpose of your essay in a clear thesis statement. Using the ideas you have written by brainstorming, write a sentence that tells what your essay is about.

Hint: Will you be presenting a certain number of *steps* in your how-to essay? Or will you be explaining a number of different *ways* to paint the exterior of a house? Your thesis statement will reveal your presentation plan.

Organizing your Ideas

After you have written a strong thesis statement telling what your essay is about, look at the ideas you have generated by brainstorming and identify the ones that best support your thesis statement. When writing an expository essay, it is sometimes helpful to make an outline to help you organize your ideas. For example, your outline might look something like this:

How to Paint the Exterior of a House

I. Preparation
   A. Dressing appropriately
      1. Old clothes and shoes
      2. Hat that covers hair
   B. Gathering materials
      1. Sandpaper
      2. Exterior primer
      3. Exterior paint
      4. Brush and/or roller
      5. Masking tape
      6. Rags

II. Process
   A. Preparing the surface
      1. Sanding
      2. Cleaning
      3. Masking
   B. Priming the surfaces
      1. Walls
      2. Trim
      3. Window sills
      4. Doors
   C. Painting the surfaces
      1. Walls
      2. Trim
      3. Window sills
      4. Doors

III. Afterward
   A. Clean-up of painting supplies
   B. Removal of masking tape

For this assignment, you may either use the outline above, or you may create your own outline or thought clusters based on the ideas you generated while brainstorming. If you choose to use an outline, each Roman numeral part of your outline will represent a body paragraph to be developed later. You should have at least three of these.

Tone   The **tone** of an essay reflects the writer's attitude toward the topic. Your attitude can be formal or informal, sarcastic or straight-forward, serious or silly, admiring or critical. Before you begin writing, you must decide on your tone.

Forming Topic Sentences   Once you have decided on your tone, selected the main ideas from your brainstorming, and arranged them in clusters or an outline, take those ideas and form them into topic sentences. Each topic sentence will become a main idea for your essay's body paragraphs.

Practice   Write a thesis statement and at least three topic sentences that clearly explain your thesis statement. In Lesson 12, we shall develop these topic sentences into body paragraphs and then complete the expository essay.

THESIS STATEMENT: _____

_____

_____

Topic sentence: _____

_____

_____

Topic sentence: _____

_____

_____

Topic sentence: _____

_____

_____

LESSON 12

Writing an Expository Essay

In Lesson 11, you prepared to write your expository essay about how to paint the exterior of a house. By brainstorming, you gathered ideas and wrote a thesis statement. You chose the best of those ideas and put them into clusters or an outline to create a logical order, or organization, for your presentation. Then you used the main ideas to create at least three topic sentences. Now you are ready to write the complete essay.

Practice Using the topic sentences you wrote for Lesson 11, follow the steps below to complete the expository essay.

1. For each topic sentence, write a body paragraph to support the thesis statement. Refer to your notes or outline and use the ideas underneath each Roman numeral to write body sentences that further explain, or expand, each topic sentence.

2. Create an introductory paragraph and a concluding paragraph. Remember that the introductory sentence should grab the reader's interest and that the "last words" of your conclusion will leave a lasting impression.

3. Add transitions between body paragraphs to make your ideas easier for the reader to follow. Transitions that indicate order, such as "the first step..." or "the second step...," are appropriate in a how-to essay. Pay special attention to the transition into the concluding paragraph.

4. Finally, put all the parts together to form a complete essay. As you are working, make any necessary corrections to your previous work. You might add things, take things out, or make any other change that results in a clearer, easier-to-follow expository essay.

Additional Practice (Optional) After you have evaluated your expository essay using the guidelines in Lesson 13, you might try writing another expository essay on a topic of your choice or on one of these topics:

1. Explain how to play a game, any game with which you are familiar.

2. Write an essay giving at least three reasons why you are thankful to be living in the United States of America.

3. Give instructions for making a salad, main dish, or dessert that you like.

4. Introduce your reader to an interesting person, such as one of your relatives, family members, or friends.

5. Write an essay about the proper care and feeding of an animal that you are familiar with.

6. Explain in detail how one might decorate a yard or room for a friend's birthday party.

7. Compare and contrast the rat and the mouse.

8. Tell how to construct a kite, paper airplane, or some other craft of your choice.

9. Compare and contrast the typical personality of a dog versus a cat.

10. Write instructions for checking the weather forecast on the internet. Assume that your audience is completely unfamiliar with the computer.

Evaluating the Expository Essay

We remember that all of our writing is "work in progress." The knowledge that *writing is a process* guides our thinking throughout the construction of an essay. Throughout the steps of brainstorming, organizing our thoughts, creating body paragraphs, and adding transitions, we constantly make changes to improve our work.

Evaluating Your Writing

In Lesson 12, you completed your expository essay. Now that some time has passed, you are ready to evaluate it using the following guidelines.

Ask yourself these questions:

• Is my introductory sentence interesting? *If it is not interesting to you, it certainly will not be interesting to the reader.*

• Does my thesis statement clearly state what my essay is about?

• Does each body paragraph have a clear topic sentence at the beginning that tells the reader exactly what the paragraph will be about? *Read each topic sentence without the rest of the paragraph to see if it can stand alone as a strong idea.*

• Does each of my topic sentences strongly support my thesis statement?

• Are there other details, facts, examples, or steps, that I can add to help improve my explanation or help the reader to better follow my instructions?

• Are my sentences in a logical or practical order?

• Does each paragraph (except for the first) begin with an effective transition?

• Are there other details that I can add as additional body paragraphs to create a fuller or clearer explanation?

• Are some of my sentences weak or confusing? Should they be removed because they do not help me to explain?

- Do my body paragraphs appear in the best possible order? Could I place them in a different order that is more logical or effective?

- Is each sentence constructed as well as it should be? *Read each sentence in each paragraph as if it were the only sentence on the page. This helps you to catch sentence fragments, run-on sentences, misspellings, and grammatical errors.*

- Does my concluding paragraph summarize and reinforce the ideas expressed in the essay?

Practice Use the Evaluation Form on the page following this lesson to evaluate the expository essay you wrote for Lesson 12. Read your essay carefully as you check for the items listed on the Evaluation Form. Write YES or NO in the blank next to each question.

When you are finished, you will either be confident that you have a strong essay, or you will know where it needs to be improved.

If you answered NO to one or more of the questions on the Evaluation Form, rewrite to improve those areas.

When you can answer YES to every question on the Evaluation Form, you will have completed this assignment.

Expository Essay Evaluation Form

Thesis: _____

_____ Is my introductory sentence interesting? *If it is not interesting to you, it certainly won't be interesting to the reader.*

_____ Do I have a thesis statement that clearly explains the subject of this essay?

_____ Does my thesis statement clearly state my method of presentation?

_____ Does each body paragraph have a clear topic sentence at the beginning that tells the reader exactly what the paragraph will be about? *Read each topic sentence without the rest of the paragraph to see if it can stand alone as a strong idea.*

_____ Have I included every detail, fact, or example that I can to help improve my explanation and help the reader to better understand my point?

_____ Within each paragraph, are my sentences in a logical or practical order?

_____ Does each paragraph (except for the first paragraph) begin with an effective transition?

_____ Have I included every idea that I can add as an additional body paragraph to create a fuller or clearer explanation?

_____ Are all of my sentences strong and clear? Do they all help me to explain?

_____ Do my body paragraphs appear in the best possible order? Is their order logical and effective?

_____ Is each sentence structured as well as it could be? *Read each sentence in each paragraph as if it were the only sentence on the page. This helps you catch fragments and run-on sentences and evaluate the overall strength or weakness of each sentence.*

_____ Does my concluding paragraph summarize and reinforce the ideas expressed in the essay?

LESSON 14

Developing an Outline

We have learned that an outline can help us to organize our ideas for an expository essay. In an outline, we can arrange and sequence thoughts in a logical manner.

In this lesson, we shall review the basic outline form and practice developing an outline from an essay we have already written. This exercise will give us confidence in our ability to make an outline in preparation for writing future essays or research papers.

Outline Form An **outline** is a list of topics and subtopics arranged in an organized form.

- We use Roman numerals (I, II, III) for main topics.
- We use uppercase letters (A, B, C,) for subtopics, or different parts of our main ideas.
- We use lowercase letters (a, b, c) to show even smaller parts.
- For a very detailed outline we use alternating numbers and letters as shown below.

Title

I. Main topic
   A. Subtopic of I
   B. Subtopic of I
      1. Subtopic of B
      2. Subtopic of B
         a. Subtopic of 2
         b. Subtopic of 2
            (1) Subtopic of b
            (2) Subtopic of b
               (a) Subtopic of (2)
               (b) Subtopic of (2)
II. Main topic
   A. Etc.
      1. Etc.

Notice that we indent subtopics so that all letters or numbers of the same kind will come directly under one another in a vertical line.

Topic Outline An outline may be either a topic outline or a sentence outline. In a **topic outline** each main topic or subtopic is written as a single word or phrase. Below is an example of a topic outline of the first part of an essay on objections to chores.

Chore Boredom

I. Why doing chores is necessary
   A. To share the family workload
   B. To demonstrate responsibility and maturity

II. Why some chores are boring
   A. Too monotonous
   B. Take time away from pleasurable activity

Sentence Outline After you have created a topic outline, you can add more words and descriptions to each item to create a **sentence outline.** In a sentence outline each topic is expressed as a complete sentence. Notice how the sentence outline below communicates more meaning than the short phrases of the topic outline.

Chore Boredom

I. Doing chores is necessary.
   A. We share the family workload as we do chores.
   B. We demonstrate responsibility and maturity by doing chores.

II. Some chores are boring.
   A. Monotonous chores are boring.
   B. Chores take time away from pleasurable activity.

Practice On a separate sheet of paper, practice the outlining process by organizing the following set of information in a topic outline form. First, look carefully over the list below. You will find *two* main topics (I. and II.) each having *four* subtopics (A., B., C., and D.). You might begin by circling the two main topics.

descriptive	haiku
free verse	narrative
poetry types	expository
persuasive	limerick
sonnet	essay types

Your outline will look like this:

I. _____
   A. _____
   B. _____
   C. _____
   D. _____
II. _____
   A. _____
   B. _____
   C. _____
   D. _____

Additional Practice

Answers for this practice are found on the last page of the writing packet.

Practice the outlining process by organizing the following set of information in a topic outline form. First circle the main topic and then underline the three main subtopics. You can then make a simple outline. Put the main topic as Roman numeral (I) and the three main subtopics as letters (A, B, C). You can place the smaller subtopics as numbers (1, 2, 3).

Former governor of Texas   Freed the slaves

Abraham Lincoln   Father of our country

Gettysburg Address   George Washington

Twenty-first century President   American Presidents

Chopped down a cherry tree   George W. Bush

Hint:

I. _____
  A. _____
    1. _____
    2. _____
  B. _____
    1. _____
    2. _____
  C. _____
    1. _____
    2. _____

Additional Practice

For Lesson 4, you wrote a complete essay containing at least three body paragraphs. Create a topic outline covering the body paragraphs of that essay. Hint: The topic sentence of each body paragraph will become a word or phrase beside a Roman numeral indicating a main topic in your outline. Therefore, your outline will have at least three Roman numerals.

Additional Practice

(Optional) For Lesson 8, you wrote a persuasive essay containing at least three body paragraphs. Create a topic outline for this essay.

LESSON 15

Preparing to Write a Research Paper: The Working Bibliography

A research paper is a type of expository writing based on information gathered from a variety of reliable sources. In the future, you may be asked to write a research paper for an English, history, science, art, or music class. Knowing the procedure for writing a good research paper will help you to become a successful high school and college student.

In this lesson, we shall learn how to prepare for writing a research paper on an assigned subject. To practice the procedure, you may choose one of the following subjects:

1. The Morgan Horse, Choice of the U.S. Cavalry

2. How the Electoral College Works

3. Ronald Reagan's Main Accomplishments as President

4. President John F. Kennedy's Most Important Contributions

5. A subject of your choice

Tone The research paper requires a serious tone. The writing should be formal and impersonal. Therefore, we do not use first person pronouns, such as *I, me,* or *my.*

Gathering Sources of Information The first step in researching your subject is to compile a **working bibliography,** a collection of possible sources of information. Consider the following possibilities of sources that you might use:

- traditional library research aids including card catalog, *Readers' Guide,* and reference works

- on-line electronic databases and on-line reference works such as electronic encyclopedias

- internet web sites

- government publications

- personal interviews or correspondence

- museums

- scholarly journals

Using your Library's Resources

Today all public and private libraries have many non-traditional sources of information that you may not see when you first walk in the door. They are not on shelves; instead, they are on computer networks.

Virtually every library, even the small local one, now subscribes to special on-line databases and information providing services. These sources come in a wide variety in terms of the type of information they provide and the level of the information.

Go to your librarian and explain exactly what type of information you want to find, and he or she will show you on the library computers how to find that information.

Evaluating Sources of Information

Not all sources are reliable or useful. We must evaluate each source for its usefulness. Asking the following questions will help us to evaluate each source:

1. *Is the information current?* A 1970 study of smog in large cities is out-of-date. Therefore, it would not be an appropriate source for a paper on today's pollution problems except for drawing comparisons with the past. Generally, a source should not be more than ten years old.

2. *Is the source objective and impartial?* An article written by the president of Mountain Spring Bottled Water about impurities in local well water might not be an objective source. The author could be trying to sell you something.

3. *For what audience was the source intended?* Material written for young children might be over-simplified while material written for specialists might be too technical.

4. *Is the person who wrote the information credible?* Material written either by scholars who work at universities or colleges, or by people who have worked for many years in a related field and are known to have done recognized work, is more likely to be believed than material authored by someone who has published no work before, has no experience in the area, or who has not obtained a college degree.

5. *Are there other sources that agree?* Do you find more than one source that agrees with the information you have found? If you fine one source that totally disagrees with all others, you may want to look for more evidence before using that single source.

Preparing Bibliography Cards

After gathering sources, evaluating each one for its usefulness, and choosing only those that are appropriate, we are ready to compile a working bibliography, the list of sources from which we will glean information for our research paper.

We can record each source on a separate three-by-five index card or on a word processing document on our computer, including all the information listed below. We will need this information later to prepare our final Bibliography when our paper is completed.

BOOKS

Include the following on your index card or word processing document:

1. Author's (or editor's) full name, last name first. Indicate editor by placing *ed.* after the name. If the book has more than one author, only the first author is written last name first. Others are written first name first.

2. Title and subtitle underlined

3. City of publication

4. Publisher's name

5. Most recent copyright year.

MAGAZINE, NEWSPAPER, JOURNAL, AND ENCYCLOPEDIA ARTICLES

Include the following on your index card or word processing document:

1. Author's (or editor's) full name, last name first. Indicate editor by placing <u>ed.</u> after the name. If the article has more than one author, only the first author is written last name first. Others are written first name first.

2. Title of article in quotation marks

3. Name of magazine, newspaper, journal, or encyclopedia underlined

4. Date and page numbers of *magazines*
   Date, edition, section, page numbers of *newspapers*
   Volume, year, page numbers of *journals*
   Edition and year of *encyclopedias*

We assign each bibliography card a "source number" and write it in the upper left corner. Later we will use this number to identify the sources of our notes. Below are some sample bibliography cards.

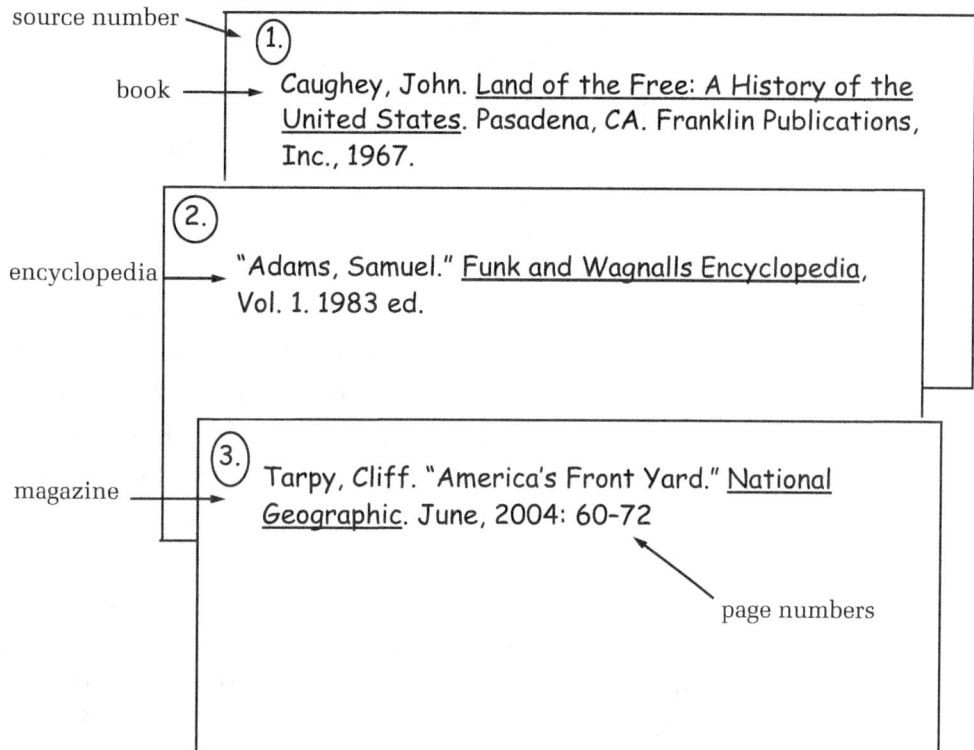

source number → 1.
book → Caughey, John. <u>Land of the Free: A History of the United States</u>. Pasadena, CA. Franklin Publications, Inc., 1967.

2.
encyclopedia → "Adams, Samuel." <u>Funk and Wagnalls Encyclopedia</u>, Vol. 1. 1983 ed.

3.
magazine → Tarpy, Cliff. "America's Front Yard." <u>National Geographic</u>. June, 2004: 60–72

page numbers

Practice After you have chosen a subject from the list of suggestions for your research paper, follow the instructions in this lesson for gathering and evaluating sources and for preparing bibliography cards. Locate at least *five* appropriate sources and prepare a bibliography card for each one. Remember to assign each card a source number and write it in the upper left corner.

If you are using a computer instead of index cards, you may list your sources below so that your teacher can review them.

AUTHOR   TITLE

Source Number

#1 _____

#2 _____

#3 _____

#4 _____

#5 _____

Preparing to Write a Research Paper: Notes, Thesis, Outline

In Lesson 15, you chose a subject for a research paper and created a working bibliography, at least four sources of information that you will use for your paper. In this lesson, you will take notes from these sources, organize your notes, create a thesis statement, and develop an outline for your paper.

Taking Notes It is helpful to use something for taking notes that is easily recognizable as different from the three-by-five cards you used for your bibliography cards. You could use four-by-six inch cards or different colored cards for taking notes. If you are working on a computer, save your notes as a different document from your bibliography.

As you read through your sources, write down information that specifically applies to your subject. Write most of your notes in your own words. You may summarize the author's main ideas, or you may record specific facts or details in your own words. If you quote the author, you must enclose the author's exact words in quotation marks.

Beware of Plagiarism! Whenever you take notes from a source, you must give credit to that source, whether you quote exactly from an author or use your own words. **Failing to give an author credit for his or her ideas is called *plagiarism.*** *Plagiarism* is intellectual theft; it is against the law, for it is just as unacceptable as material theft. People who *plagiarize,* or steal other people's ideas, find themselves subject to expulsion from high school and college courses. (For practice in avoiding plagiarism, see Lesson 33.) Therefore, you must carefully give credit to authors and sources that you use in your research paper even if you reword, or paraphrase, the information.

In the upper right corner of your note card, you will enter the source number from your working bibliography. If you are on a computer, put the source number in parentheses at the beginning of the note.

At the end of each note, write the page or pages on which you found the information.

Below is a sample note card.

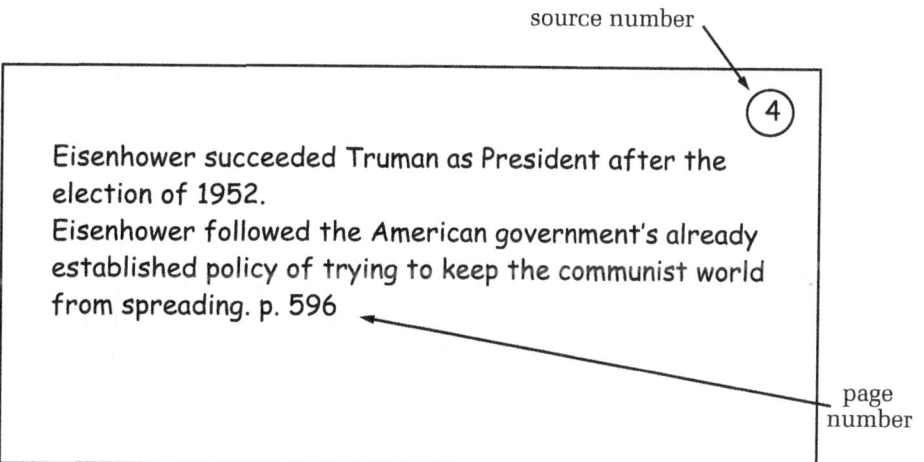

Organizing Your Information After you have taken notes on all your sources and gathered sufficient information for your research paper, take some time to organize your note cards and arrange them in a logical order. These cards represent your brainstorming ideas. Now, instead of having ideas written around a circle, you have them on note cards. If you are using a computer, you can copy and paste your notes in different orders to see which order seems logical.

Thesis Statement Now look over your organized notes and write a thesis statement that clearly explains the main idea of your research paper.

Outline In Lesson 14, you learned to develop an outline. Use your organized note cards to help you create an informal topic outline for your research paper. This outline will guide you as you begin to write the first draft of your paper in the next lesson.

Practice Follow the instructions in this lesson for taking notes from your sources. Then organize your notes, write a thesis statement, and develop an outline for your research paper.

Example

Thesis
I. *Topic sentence*
   A.
   B.
      1.
      2.
II. *Topic sentence*
   A. *etc.*

LESSON 17

Writing the Research Paper

In Lesson 16, you took notes from your sources, organized your notes, wrote a thesis statement, and created an outline for your research paper.

Writing the First Draft

With your outline, your thesis statement, your notes, and your bibliography cards or computer file in front of you, you are ready to begin writing the first draft of your research paper. A first draft is a rough copy that is for your use only. It is meant to be revised again and again until you are satisfied with it.

As you write, keep in mind your thesis statement, your purpose, and the need for a formal tone. Use the information from your notes to support your thesis and to fill in the details as you follow your outline for organization.

Create an introductory paragraph that captures the reader's attention. Consider beginning with an interesting statement, an anecdote, or an example. Make certain that your opening paragraph includes your thesis statement.

Use the main points in your outline to create topic sentences for your body paragraphs. Then develop these topic sentences into paragraphs, making sure that all of your information relates to your thesis statement.

Pay special attention to transitions as you begin each new paragraph.

Your concluding paragraph will summarize and reinforce the ideas set forth in the rest of your research paper.

Documentation of Sources

Writing the first draft of a research paper involves bringing together information from your different sources, which you must acknowledge properly. We call this acknowledgement the **documentation** of sources.

As you write, you must credit your sources for both ideas and quotations. There are various methods of documenting sources for research papers. In this book, we shall practice a method called *parenthetical citations*. This form identifies sources in parentheses that are placed as close as possible to the ideas or quotations we are using. Inside the parentheses, we place a reference to the source in our Bibliography, which is found at the end of the research paper.

Usually, the reference inside the parentheses consists only of an author's last name and the page number from which the material was taken. For example, (Caughey 191) would appear right after an idea taken from page one hundred ninety-one in John Caughey's book, which is listed in the Bibliography.

When no author and only a title is given for a source, we place a shortened form of the title and the page number or numbers in the parentheses: ("Freedom" 213).

Notice that the end punctuation for a sentence containing borrowed material is placed *after* the parenthetical citation:

> "What was revolutionary about Jefferson's coming into office was that there was no revolution" (Caughey 191).

punctuation mark

The highly respected Modern Language Association (MLA) gives us many more detailed guidelines for parenthetical citations. However, in this lesson we shall follow the simplified instructions above.

The Bibliography The bibliography, the list of the sources that you used as you wrote your paper, comes at the end of the research paper.

Follow these steps to create your bibliography:

1. Alphabetize your bibliography cards or computer entries according to the last names of the authors or the first important word in a title if there is no author.

2. Copy the information from all of your alphabetized bibliography cards under the title "Bibliography" or "Works Cited."

3. Indent all lines after the first line of each entry and punctuate as shown in the example below.

Bibliography

Flattery, Pearl. "How to Please your Constituents." <u>Better Image Journal</u>, October, 2005: 17–23.

Shrewd, David. <u>A Study in Campaign Strategies</u>. New York, Hilldale Publishers, 2004.

In high school and college, you will learn to follow more detailed guidelines given by MLA for bibliographic entries.

However, in this lesson you may follow the simplified instructions above unless your teacher advises you to do otherwise.

Practice Follow the procedure given in this lesson for writing the first draft of your research paper, documenting your sources, and making your bibliography.

Evaluating the Research Paper

The knowledge that *writing is a process* guides our thinking throughout the construction of our research paper. From the first steps in choosing our subject, to gathering information and organizing our thoughts, to creating body paragraphs, to adding transitions, we constantly make changes to improve our work.

Evaluating Your Writing

In Lesson 17, you completed the first draft of your research paper. Now that some time has passed, you are ready to evaluate it using the following guidelines.

Ask yourself these questions:

- Are my sources reliable, objective, and current?

- Is my introductory sentence interesting? *If it is not interesting to you, it certainly will not be interesting to the reader.*

- Does my thesis clearly state the purpose of my paper?

- Does the beginning of the research paper clearly establish a formal, serious tone?

- Does each body paragraph have a clear topic sentence at the beginning that tells the reader exactly what the paragraph will be about? *Read each topic sentence without the rest of the paragraph to see if it can stand alone as a strong idea.*

- Does each paragraph include specific details and examples from my research?

- Have I correctly documented each piece of borrowed information?

- Are my sentences in a logical order?

- Does each paragraph (except for the first) begin with an effective transition?

- Are there other details that I can add as additional body paragraphs to create a fuller or more complete paper?

- Are some of my sentences weak or confusing? Should they be removed because they do not relate to my thesis?

- Do my body paragraphs appear in the best possible order? Could I place them in a different order that is more logical or effective?

- Is each sentence constructed as well as it should be? *Read each sentence in each paragraph as if it were the only sentence on the page. This helps you to catch sentence fragments, run-on sentences, misspellings, and grammatical errors.*

- Does my ending paragraph obviously conclude my presentation? Does it reinforce my thesis statement?

Practice   Use the Evaluation Form on the page following this lesson to evaluate the research paper you wrote for Lesson 17. Read your research paper carefully as you check for the items listed on the Evaluation Form. Write YES or NO in the blank next to each question.

When you are finished, you will either be confident that you have a strong research paper, or you will know where it needs to be improved.

If you answered NO to one or more of the questions on the Evaluation Form, rewrite to improve those areas.

When you can answer YES to every question on the Evaluation Form, you will have completed this assignment.

Research Paper Evaluation Form

Subject: _____

_____ Are my sources reliable, objective, and current?

_____ Is my introductory sentence interesting? *If it is not interesting to you, it certainly will not be interesting to the reader.*

_____ Does the beginning of the research paper clearly establish a formal, serious tone?

_____ Does the thesis clearly state the purpose of the paper?

_____ Does each body paragraph have a clear topic sentence at the beginning that tells the reader exactly what the paragraph will be about? *Read each topic sentence without the rest of the paragraph to see if it can stand alone as a strong idea.*

_____ Do the details all contribute to the reader's understanding of the thesis?

_____ Within each paragraph, are my sentences in a logical or practical order?

_____ Does each paragraph (except for the first paragraph) begin with an effective transition?

_____ Is each piece of borrowed material properly documented? Have I credited each of my sources?

_____ Are all of my sentences strong and clear? Do they all directly relate to the thesis?

_____ Do my body paragraphs appear in the best possible order? Is their order logical and effective?

_____ Is each sentence structured as well as it could be? *Read each sentence in each paragraph as if it were the only sentence on the page. This helps you catch fragments and run-on sentences and evaluate the overall strength or weakness of each sentence.*

_____ Does my concluding paragraph summarize my research and reinforce my thesis statement?

Personal Narrative

Narrative writing tells a story or relates a series of events. In a **personal narrative,** the writer tells a story about a significant personal experience or event.

In this lesson, you will prepare to write a personal narrative in which you will share your feelings about how an experience affected you or taught you something.

Since this will be a personal narrative—a story that happened to you—you will be writing in what is called "the first person." Writing in the first person is just as if you were telling one of your friends about something that happened to you at school yesterday. You will be using "I" and "we," and you can include action, suspense, vivid description, and even dialogue.

Choosing a Personal Experience

To think of an experience for a personal narrative that you would like to share, consider the following:

- a wonderful (or disastrous) first time that you did something

- a memorable struggle or hardship that you experienced

- a "turning point" in your life

- an interesting, exciting, humorous, or moving event in your life

- an unusual or once-in-a-life-time experience, such as touring a distant country, meeting a famous person, or making an amazing discovery

Reading through the daily journals that you have written might give you additional ideas.

Brainstorming

On a piece of scratch paper, quickly write every experience that comes to your mind. When you have finished, select the one that you think is most interesting and write it on another piece of paper.

After selecting the experience you plan to write about in your personal narrative, begin brainstorming in order to recall details or emotions about this experience. List all words and phrases that come to mind. Without concern for spelling or grammar, write everything that occurs to you.

Organizing your Information Once you have gathered your thoughts and memories, begin to plan your narrative by organizing the events in a logical order, which might be chronological order—the sequence in which the events occurred. Your rough plan might look something like this:

First: For my science project I was building batteries from pieces of metal and different fruits and vegetables, and...

Then: My guinea pig escaped from its cage and ate most of the fruits and vegetables, and...

Then: I discovered that my project was ruined and...

Then: My sister helped me rebuild the batteries and...

Finally: I learned to appreciate my sister, my helpful friend.

Practice For your personal narrative, write a rough plan similar to the one above. In the next lesson, you will expand each part of this plan into a paragraph and complete your narrative by filling in detail, action, and dialogue.

First: _____

_____

Then: _____

_____

Then: _____

_____

Then: _____

_____

Finally: _____

_____

Writing a Personal Narrative

In Lesson 19, you chose an interesting personal experience and created a rough plan for writing a personal narrative. In this lesson, you will use your rough plan and any other notes and begin writing your narrative.

Opening Paragraph Remember that your opening paragraph should capture the interest of the reader and establish your tone, which reveals your feelings or attitudes about the experience. You will write in first person, using the pronoun *I* or *we*.

Body Paragraphs Although you have a plan to follow, you may alter it as you write. Following the opening paragraph, each "then" part of your rough plan might become the topic sentence for a body paragraph in which you fill in details, actions, and any necessary dialogue.

Concluding Paragraph Your concluding paragraph will include a personal summary or commentary about how the experience affected you or taught you something significant.

Practice Write your personal narrative according to the guidelines above. Include an opening paragraph, two or more body paragraphs, and a concluding paragraph.

Evaluating the Personal Narrative

All of our writing is "work in progress." The knowledge that *writing is a process* guides our thinking throughout the construction of our personal narrative. From the first steps in selecting an experience to share, to organizing our thoughts, to creating body paragraphs, to adding transitions, we constantly make changes to improve our work.

Evaluating Your Writing

In Lesson 20, you completed your personal narrative. Now that some time has passed, you are ready to evaluate it using the following guidelines.

Ask yourself these questions:

- Is my introductory sentence interesting? *If it is not interesting to you, it certainly will not be interesting to the reader.*

- Does the beginning of the narrative clearly establish the tone?

- Does each body paragraph have a clear topic sentence at the beginning that tells the reader exactly what the paragraph will be about? *Read each topic sentence without the rest of the paragraph to see if it can stand alone as a strong idea.*

- Is the first-person point of view consistently maintained throughout the narrative?

- Are there other details, descriptions, emotions, or dialogue I could add to make a more interesting narrative?

- Are my sentences in a logical or chronological order?

- Does each paragraph (except for the first) begin with an effective transition?

- Are there other details that I can add as additional body paragraphs to create a fuller or more complete narrative?

- Are some of my sentences weak or confusing? Should they be removed because they do not relate to the story?

- Do my body paragraphs appear in the best possible order? Could I place them in a different order that is more logical or effective?

- Is each sentence constructed as well as it should be? *Read each sentence in each paragraph as if it were the only sentence on the page. This helps you to catch sentence fragments, run-on sentences, misspellings, and grammatical errors.*

- Does my concluding paragraph contain a summary or commentary about how the experience affected me?

Practice Use the Evaluation Form on the page following this lesson to evaluate the personal narrative you wrote for Lesson 20. Read your narrative carefully as you check for the items listed on the Evaluation Form. Write YES or NO in the blank next to each question.

When you are finished, you will either be confident that you have a strong personal narrative, or you will know where it needs to be improved.

If you answered NO to one or more of the questions on the Evaluation Form, rewrite to improve those areas.

When you can answer YES to every question on the Evaluation Form, you will have completed this assignment.

Personal Narrative Evaluation Form

Title: _____

_____ Is my introductory sentence interesting? *If it is not interesting to you, it certainly won't be interesting to the reader.*

_____ Does the beginning of the narrative clearly establish the tone?

_____ Is the first-person point of view consistently maintained throughout the narrative?

_____ Does each body paragraph have a clear topic sentence at the beginning that tells the reader exactly what the paragraph will be about? *Read each topic sentence without the rest of the paragraph to see if it can stand alone as a strong idea.*

_____ Do the details all contribute to the reader's understanding of my personal experience?

_____ Within each paragraph, are my sentences in a logical or practical order?

_____ Does each paragraph (except for the first paragraph) begin with an effective transition?

_____ Have I included every detail that I can add as an additional body paragraph to create a fuller or more complete narrative?

_____ Are all of my sentences strong and clear? Do they all directly relate to the story?

_____ Do my body paragraphs appear in the best possible order? Is their order logical and effective?

_____ Is each sentence structured as well as it could be? *Read each sentence in each paragraph as if it were the only sentence on the page. This helps you catch fragments and run-on sentences and evaluate the overall strength or weakness of each sentence.*

_____ Does my concluding paragraph contain a personal summary or commentary about how the experience affected me or taught me something?

Preparing to Write a Descriptive Essay

Descriptive writing describes a person, place, object, or event. With language that appeals to the senses, descriptive writing creates pictures in the reader's mind. Strong, vivid, and precise words are essential in creating clear descriptions.

In this lesson, we shall discuss the use of modifiers, comparisons, and sensory expressions to create accurate and complete descriptions. Then you will prepare to write a descriptive essay about a person whom you can observe as you are writing.

Modifiers   To add detail, we can use modifiers—adjectives and adverbs, phrases and clauses. Modifiers supply additional information, making nouns and verbs more specific and precise.

> *Curious* yet *timid*, *six-year-old* Rosita *cautiously* lifted the box lid and peeked inside.

Comparisons   In addition to modifiers, we can use comparisons to make a description more vivid. *Simile* and *metaphor* are two kinds of comparisons. A **simile** expresses similarity between two things by using the word *like* or *as*:

> *Like* a polliwog, little Timmy wiggled across the deep end of the swimming pool.

A **metaphor**, on the other hand, describes one thing as though it were another thing:

> Wiggly little Timmy *was a polliwog* in the swimming pool.

Both comparisons, simile and metaphor, help the reader to see a fuller picture of the little swimmer.

Sensory Expressions   To create a more vivid image, we can appeal to the reader's five senses by detailing things that one can see, hear, smell, taste, and touch. For example, we can hear a goose *honk,* see a distant light *glimmer,* smell the *noxious odor* of a skunk, feel the *smoothness* of a polished stone, and taste the *sour* lemon that purses our lips.

Below, Rudyard Kipling uses details, modifiers, and comparisons to describe an old man in his novel *Kim*.

> He was nearly six feet high, dressed in fold upon fold of dingy stuff like horse-blanketing, and not one fold of it could Kim refer to any known trade or profession. At his belt hung a long open-work iron pencase and a wooden rosary such as holy men wear. On his head was a gigantic sort of tam-o'-shanter. His face was yellow and wrinkled, like that of Fook Shing, the Chinese bootmaker in the bazar. His eyes turned up at the corners and looked like little slits of onyx.

In *The Grapes of Wrath*, John Steinbeck uses similes to describe the aftermath of an Oklahoma dust storm:

> In the morning dust hung like fog, and the sun was as red as ripe new blood.

Here Steinbeck uses a simile to create a picture of a man's fingernails:

> His hands were hard, with broad fingers and nails as thick and ridged as little clam shells.

In her novel *Johnny Tremain*, Esther Forbes uses metaphor and sensory images to describe a place:

> Boston slowly opened its eyes, stretched, and woke. The sun struck in horizontally from the east, flashing upon weathervanes—brass cocks and arrows, here a glass-eyed Indian, there a copper grasshopper—and the bells in the steeples cling-clanged, telling the people it was time to be up and about.

In the same novel, the author goes on to describe Johnny Tremain:

> Johnny was already in his leather breeches, pulling on his coarse shirt, tucking in the tails. He was a rather skinny boy, neither large nor small for fourteen. He had a thin, sleep-flushed face, light eyes, a wry mouth, and fair, lank hair. Although two years younger than the swinish Dove, inches shorter, pounds lighter, he knew, and old Mr. Lapham knew, busy Mrs. Lapham and her four daughters and Dove and Dusty also knew, that Johnny Tremain was boss of the attic, and almost of the house.

The examples above show how authors can create vivid pictures using details, modifiers, comparisons, and sensory expressions.

Brainstorming After choosing one person whom you can observe as you write, you are ready to begin brainstorming in order to gather precise and concrete details that will appeal to the reader's senses and fully describe that person.

You might want to consider these aspects of the person:

1. Physical appearance—size, age, gender; colors, shapes, and textures of hair, eyes, skin, and clothing; peculiar features or facial expressions; movements and gestures

2. Personality traits—mannerisms, habits, usual disposition. By their actions, people may demonstrate that they are intense or relaxed, hyperactive or laid-back, outgoing or shy, humble or proud, etc.

3. How the person affects others and the world around him or her—Where does the person live? What does the person do? What are his or her passions or interests? How does he or she relate to others? How does this person make you or other people feel?

On a blank piece of paper, quickly write everything that comes to your mind concerning the person you wish to describe. Without regard for spelling or grammar, write all the nouns, verbs, adjectives, adverbs, phrases, clauses, comparisons, and sensory expressions that occur to you.

Organizing your Information Once you have gathered your thoughts and observations, begin to plan your descriptive essay by grouping the words and phrases into clusters. You might have one cluster of words and phrases that describe the person's physical appearance, another cluster focusing on the person's personality, and another telling about what the person does and/or how the person affects others and the world around him or her.

You can use each idea cluster to develop a topic sentence for each body paragraph in your essay.

Thesis Statement In your essay, you will be describing many different aspects of one person. What is the main impression you want your reader to receive concerning this person? Your thesis statement will sum up that which is most important.

Practice For your descriptive essay, write a thesis statement and three or more topic sentences about the person you wish to describe. In the next lesson, you will develop each topic sentence into a body paragraph by adding more detail. Keep your brainstorming paper and this assignment in your folder or binder so that you will be ready to complete your essay.

THESIS STATEMENT: _____

_____

_____

Topic sentence: _____

_____

_____

Topic sentence: _____

_____

_____

Topic sentence: _____

_____

_____

Writing a Descriptive Essay

In Lesson 22, you prepared to write your descriptive essay about a person of your choice. By brainstorming, you gathered ideas and details. Then you organized those details into clusters representing main ideas. From those clusters, you created a thesis statement and at least three topic sentences. Now you are ready to write the complete essay.

Practice   Using the topic sentences you wrote for Lesson 22, follow the steps below to complete the expository essay.

1. Develop each topic sentence into a body paragraph, keeping your thesis in mind. Refer to your brainstorming notes and idea clusters to write body sentences that add more detail and create a vivid picture in the reader's mind.

2. Create an introductory paragraph and a concluding paragraph. Remember that the introductory sentence should grab the reader's interest and that the "last words" of your conclusion will leave a lasting impression.

3. Add transitions between body paragraphs to make your ideas easier for the reader to follow. Pay special attention to the transition into the concluding paragraph.

4. Finally, put all the parts together to form a complete essay. As you are working, make any necessary corrections to your previous work. You might add things, take things out, or make any other change that results in a clearer, fuller descriptive essay.

Additional Practice   (Optional) After you have evaluated your descriptive essay using the guidelines in Lesson 24, you might try writing another descriptive essay on a topic of your choice or on one of these topics:

1. A character from a novel you have read

2. A room in your house or apartment

3. A pet, or an animal that interests you

4. An interesting or beautiful outdoor scene

5. A sporting event, birthday party, or other kind of celebration

Evaluating the Descriptive Essay

Because *writing is a process* and all of our writing is "work in progress," we constantly make changes to improve our work.

Evaluating Your Writing

In Lesson 23, you completed your descriptive essay. Now that some time has passed, you are ready to evaluate it using the following guidelines.

Ask yourself these questions:

- Is my introductory sentence interesting? *If it is not interesting to you, it certainly will not be interesting to the reader.*

- Does the thesis statement focus on a single person, place, object, or event?

- Does the thesis statement give my main impression of the person, place, object, or event that I am describing?

- Does each body paragraph have a clear topic sentence at the beginning that tells the reader exactly what the paragraph will be about? *Read each topic sentence without the rest of the paragraph to see if it can stand alone as a strong idea.*

- Are there other details, modifiers, comparisons, or sensory expressions I could add to help the reader to visualize my topic?

- Are my sentences in a logical order?

- Does each paragraph (except for the first) begin with an effective transition?

- Are there other details that I can add as additional body paragraphs to create a fuller or more complete description?

- Are some of my sentences weak or confusing? Should they be removed because they do not relate to the topic?

- Do my body paragraphs appear in the best possible order? Could I place them in a different order that is more logical or effective?

- Is each sentence constructed as well as it should be? *Read each sentence in each paragraph as if it were the only sentence on the page. This helps you to catch sentence fragments, run-on sentences, misspellings, and grammatical errors.*

- Does my concluding paragraph sum up my main impression of the person, place, object, or event?

Practice Use the Evaluation Form on the page following this lesson to evaluate the descriptive essay you wrote for Lesson 23. Read your descriptive essay carefully as you check for the items listed on the Evaluation Form. Write YES or NO in the blank next to each question.

When you are finished, you will either be confident that you have a strong descriptive essay, or you will know where it needs to be improved.

If you answered NO to one or more of the questions on the Evaluation Form, rewrite to improve those areas.

When you can answer YES to every question on the Evaluation Form, you will have completed this assignment.

Descriptive Essay Evaluation Form

Topic: _____

_____ Is my introductory sentence interesting? *If it is not interesting to you, it certainly won't be interesting to the reader.*

_____ Does the thesis statement focus on a single person, place, object, or event?

_____ Does the thesis statement give my main impression of that person, place, object, or event?

_____ Does each body paragraph have a clear topic sentence at the beginning that tells the reader exactly what the paragraph will be about? *Read each topic sentence without the rest of the paragraph to see if it can stand alone as a strong idea.*

_____ Do the details all contribute to the reader's ability to visualize or mentally experience my topic?

_____ Within each paragraph, are my sentences in a logical order?

_____ Does each paragraph (except for the first paragraph) begin with an effective transition?

_____ Have I used enough modifiers, comparisons, and sensory expressions to enable the reader to visualize my topic?

_____ Are all of my sentences strong and clear? Do they all directly relate to the topic?

_____ Do my body paragraphs appear in the best possible order? Is their order logical and effective?

_____ Is each sentence structured as well as it could be? *Read each sentence in each paragraph as if it were the only sentence on the page. This helps you catch fragments and run-on sentences and evaluate the overall strength or weakness of each sentence.*

_____ Does my concluding paragraph sum up my main impression of my topic?

We have practiced writing vivid descriptions of people, places, objects, or events using details, modifiers, comparisons, and sensory expressions. We have also written a personal narrative with dialogue, logical sentence order, and effective transitions. In this lesson, we shall use all the writing skills we have learned so far in order to create our own imaginative story.

An imaginative story is fiction; it is not a true story although it may be based on something that really happened.

Conflict, characters, setting, and plot are all parts of the imaginative story. In preparing to write our story, we shall gather information concerning each of these parts.

Conflict A short story must have a problem or situation in which struggle occurs. A character may be in conflict with another character, with the forces of nature, with the rules of society, or even with his or her own self, as an internal conflict brought about by pangs of conscience or feelings of ambivalence.

For example, notice the possible conflicts related to the two situations below.

> SITUATION 1: Wild parrots have multiplied in a Southern California town.
>
> *Conflict*: Parrots fight to protect their territory.
>
> *Conflict*: Parrots disturb people with their loud squawking.
>
> *Conflict*: People resent parrots stealing fruit and nuts from trees.

> SITUATION 2: Dr. Dimwit has locked his keys in the car at the supermarket.
>
> *Conflict*: His wife frets because he has not brought home eggs and butter for the cake she is making for guests who will arrive soon.
>
> *Conflict*: His son is waiting and waiting to be picked up from baseball practice.
>
> *Conflict*: His beeper lets him know that one of his

patients is about to deliver a baby!

To find a situation and conflict for your own imaginative story, you might talk to friends or family members, watch the news, read the newspaper, or observe what is happening in the lives of people around you.

In preparation for story-writing, spend several minutes brainstorming with the help of a friend, teacher, or family member to gather ideas of situations and conflicts. Write down all the situations and possible resulting conflicts that come to mind. Then choose the one conflict that most interests you for your imaginative story.

Tone Your attitude toward the conflict will create the **tone** of your story. The details and language you use might evoke joy, fear, amusement, grief, or some other emotion. For example, you will want your story to make the reader laugh if you feel that the situation facing the characters is funny. On the other hand, if you feel that the situation is serious and worrisome, you will try to increase the reader's anxiety.

After choosing your conflict, plan how you will establish the tone of your story by answering the following questions:

1. What is my attitude toward the conflict and the characters involved in it?

2. What details can I use to create this mood, or evoke these emotions, in the reader?

Point of View You may tell your story from either the first-person or third-person point of view.

In the first-person point of view, the story is narrated, using the pronoun *I*, by one person who either participates in or witnesses the conflict. Only the narrator's thoughts are expressed, as in the example below.

Mom just stood there staring at me with her mouth agape. Then she muttered something I couldn't understand and left the room.

In the third-person, or omniscient, point of view, the story is narrated by someone outside the story, someone who knows everything—each character's thoughts and actions. This allows the writer to reveal what any character thinks or does, as in the example below.

> *With her mouth agape, persnickety Martha just stood there staring at her son James. Then she muttered, "How can you live with this clutter?" and left the room.*

Before you begin writing your imaginative story, you must choose an appropriate point of view from which to tell about the conflict.

Characters   To create a captivating story, you must develop interesting and believable characters. Engaged in a struggle, the main character, or *protagonist*, might be opposed by another character, an *antagonist*. There may be other characters as well.

As you develop your characters, attempt to keep them consistent in their behavior and show logical reasons for any change in their behavior. For example, if an ordinarily greedy character suddenly acts generously, you must explain why.

Invent your characters by noting their physical appearances, actions, and personality traits.

Dialogue   Dialogue is the spoken words of characters. A character's words can reveal things about the character's personality, background, thoughts, and attitudes. You can use dialogue to develop your characters and make your story more interesting.

Spend a few minutes brainstorming in order to gather ideas about your main characters. Give each one a name, some physical attributes, and a distinctive personality.

Setting   The setting is the time and place of the action. Vivid, specific details help to describe the setting of a story. You must consider both location and time. Does your story take place indoors, in a specific room, or outdoors, on a mountain, beach, or prairie? Or does it take place on an airplane, boat, or train? Do the events occur in the morning, afternoon, or evening? Does the story happen in the past, present, or future?

Decide where and when your story will take place and jot down a few details that you can use later to describe your setting.

Plot The plot is the action of your story. Once you have chosen a conflict, one or more characters, and the setting of your story, you are ready to develop the action using this story plan:

> BEGINNING OF STORY
>
> > Present your characters.
> >
> > Establish the setting and tone.
> >
> > Introduce the conflict.
>
> MIDDLE OF STORY
>
> > List a series of actions that build to a climax.
>
> END OF STORY
>
> > Resolve the conflict, or show why it cannot be resolved.

Use the plan above to make notes, which you can expand later into a full imaginative story.

Practice Follow the instructions in this lesson for brainstorming, choosing a conflict, deciding on the tone and point of view, inventing characters, describing the setting, and planning the plot of your imaginative story. On a separate piece of paper, answer the following questions:

1. Who are your characters? Give a brief description of each.

2. What is the setting? Give the time and place.

3. Describe the tone, the emotions the reader will experience.

4. What is the conflict?

5. Briefly list some actions that will build to a climax.

6. How will you resolve the conflict, or show why it cannot be resolved?

Keep your answers to these questions in your folder or binder. In the next lesson, you will use this information as you write your imaginative story.

Writing an Imaginative Story

In Lesson 25, you prepared to write your imaginative story. By brainstorming, you gathered ideas and details. You chose a conflict, you decided on the tone and point of view, you invented characters, you described your setting, and you roughly planned the plot. Now you are ready to write the imaginative story.

Keep this plan in front of you as you write:

> BEGINNING OF STORY
>
> > Present your characters.
> >
> > Establish the setting and tone.
> >
> > Introduce the conflict.
>
> MIDDLE OF STORY
>
> > List a series of actions that build to a climax.
>
> END OF STORY
>
> > Resolve the conflict, or show why it cannot
> be resolved.

Practice Using your notes from Lesson 25 and the plan above, follow the steps below to write your story.

1. Write an introductory sentence that will grab the reader's attention.

2. At the beginning of the story, in whatever order you think is best, establish the setting and tone, present your characters, and introduce the conflict.

3. Add dialogue in order to reveal more about your characters' personalities, thoughts, and motivations.

4. Keep the point of view consistent throughout the story.

5. Write a series of actions that build to a climax.

6. Resolve the conflict at the end of your story, or show why it cannot be resolved.

LESSON 27

Evaluating the Imaginative Story

Because *writing is a process* and all of our writing is "work in progress," we constantly make changes to improve our work. This is especially true when writing an imaginative story. As you create your story, you may see opportunities for revisiting previous parts of your story in order to add more or different traits to a character or to alter his or her actions.

Evaluating Your Writing

In Lesson 26, you completed your imaginative story. Now that some time has passed, you are ready to evaluate it using the following guidelines.

Ask yourself these questions:

- Does my introductory sentence capture the reader's attention?

- Does the beginning of the story establish the tone and suggest the conflict?

- Are the characters believable and interesting?

- Have I revealed the characters' personalities and motivations through dialogue and action as well as description?

- Are my characters consistent in their behavior? Have I adequately explained any changes from their normal behavior?

- Are there other details, modifiers, comparisons, or sensory expressions I could add to help the reader to visualize the setting?

- Do the actions flow logically from one to another?

- Do the actions build suspense?

- Does the dialogue sound natural?

- Does the point of view remain constant throughout the story?

- Are some of my sentences weak or confusing? Should any be removed because they do not relate to the story?

- Do my sentences appear in the best possible order? Could I place them in a more logical or effective order?

- Is each sentence constructed as well as it should be? *Read each sentence in each paragraph as if it were the only sentence on the page. This helps you to catch sentence fragments, run-on sentences, misspellings, and grammatical errors.*

- Is the end of the story believable and satisfying? Has the conflict been resolved?

Practice Use the Evaluation Form on the page following this lesson to evaluate the imaginative story you wrote for Lesson 26. Read your story carefully as you check for the items listed on the Evaluation Form. Write YES or NO in the blank next to each question.

When you are finished, you will either be confident that you have a strong imaginative story, or you will know where it needs to be improved.

If you answered NO to one or more of the questions on the Evaluation Form, rewrite to improve those areas.

When you can answer YES to every question on the Evaluation Form, you will have completed this assignment.

Imaginative Story Evaluation Form

Title: _____

_____ Does my introductory sentence capture the reader's attention?

_____ Does the beginning of the story establish the tone and suggest the conflict?

_____ Are the characters believable and interesting?

_____ Have I revealed the characters' personalities and motivations through dialogue and action as well as description?

_____ Are my characters consistent in their behavior? Have I adequately explained any change from their normal behavior?

_____ Have I included sufficient details, modifiers, comparisons, and sensory expressions to enable the reader to visualize the setting?

_____ Do the actions flow logically from one to another?

_____ Do the actions build suspense?

_____ Does the dialogue sound natural?

_____ Does the point of view remain consistent throughout the story?

_____ Is each sentence strong and clear? Does each sentence relate to the story?

_____ Is each sentence structured as well as it could be? *Read each sentence in each paragraph as if it were the only sentence on the page. This helps you catch fragments and run-on sentences and evaluate the overall strength or weakness of each sentence.*

_____ Is the end of the story believable and satisfying? Has the conflict been resolved?

Writing a Chapter Summary

A summary is a relatively brief restatement of the main idea(s) in something one has read. In a summary, the writer omits details and condenses a long passage—a whole story, chapter, or book—to its main idea(s). Therefore, the summary is much shorter than the original passage.

In this lesson, we shall practice writing a one-paragraph summary of a chapter in a novel.

Chapter Summary   If you were reading a novel to a friend and if your friend fell asleep during one of the chapters, he or she might miss a great deal of the action or story line. Your brief *summary* of that missing chapter could help your friend to go on quickly to the next chapter without confusion and without rereading the entire chapter.

Example   Below is a summary of the first chapter of *The Light in the Forest* by Conrad Richter.

> True Son, a fifteen-year-old white boy, has been blissfully living with his adopted Indian father and mother for eleven years, for as long as he can remember. His white blood has been chanted away. He is a true Indian, heart and soul. Yet True Son's steadfast beliefs are challenged when he is suddenly forced to leave his Indian family. He cries out in rage as he learns he is to return to his biological white family, for he wants nothing to do with them. Darkness fills his soul as his Indian father, Cuyloga, departs from the white camp, leaving True Son behind in enemy territory.
>
> Summary by Kimberly Yan

Practice   In a single paragraph, summarize one chapter of a novel you are reading or have read in the past (or a novel from the list below). Your paragraph should not exceed eight sentences. Your summary should include major characters and provide a sense of what happens in the chapter.

Suggested novels for this exercise:

Pride and Prejudice by Jane Austen

David Copperfield by Charles Dickens

Johnny Tremain by Esther Forbes

To Kill a Mockingbird by Harper Lee

Out of the Silent Planet by C.S. Lewis

A Light in the Forest by Conrad Richter

Writing a Short Story Summary

We have learned that a summary condenses a longer passage to a shorter one, leaving out details and giving only the main ideas of the original passage.

In this lesson, we shall practice writing a one-paragraph summary of a short story.

Short Story Summary If you had read an interesting short story and wanted to tell a friend about it, you might give your friend a *summary* of the story. You would not tell the *whole* story or give away the ending. Instead, you would summarize, giving some general information about the main characters, setting, and major conflict.

Example Below is a summary of the short story "A Christmas Carol" by Charles Dickens.

> The miserly, old businessman Ebenezer Scrooge lives in nineteenth century England. On Christmas Eve, Scrooge's nephew, Fred, stops by the counting house and invites Scrooge to Christmas dinner, but Scrooge stubbornly refuses, then closes his business and goes home. Much to Scrooge's dismay, the ghost of his former business partner Jacob Marley appears to Scrooge in his bedroom and tells him he's about to be visited by three spirits in rapid succession. At the stroke of midnight the Ghost of Christmas Past appears to Scrooge, followed by the Ghost of Christmas Present and the Ghost of Christmas Yet to Be. One by one, the spirits take Scrooge on a tour through the city, visiting places and people Scrooge has known throughout his life, showing him what a wicked man he is and how badly he treats people, especially the poor, struggling Cratchit Family and their young crippled son, Tiny Tim. After witnessing these frightful past, present, and future events, will Scrooge repent of his unkind ways and make amends to those he has wronged?

Summary by Abby Grace Remington

Practice Write a one-paragraph summary of the imaginative story that you wrote for Lesson 26. Your paragraph should not exceed eight sentences. Your summary should include general information about main characters, setting, and plot.

Additional Practice Read one of the short stories suggested below or one that your teacher suggests. Then put the book away and write a one-paragraph summary of the story. Your paragraph should not exceed eight sentences. Your summary should include general information about main characters, setting, and plot.

Suggested reading:

"The Golden Fleece" by Nathaniel Hawthorne

"The Ransom of Red Chief" by O. Henry

"The Red-Headed League" by A. Conan Doyle

"A Christmas Tree" by Charles Dickens

"The Emperor's New Clothes" by Hans Christian Anderson

LESSON 30

Preparing to Write Poetry

Writing poetry allows us to tap into our imagination and experience and to use all we have learned about descriptive writing. To write a poem, we must focus our full attention on our subject in order to express impressions, emotions, and images related to it.

Through poetry, we can communicate our ideas and feelings with rhythms and repeated sounds as well as with the words we choose. In this lesson, we shall discuss traditional poetry, free verse, and some simple steps for selecting a subject and gathering thoughts in preparation for writing a poem.

Traditional Poetry

"Paul Revere's Ride" is an example of **traditional poetry,** the type of poetry established long ago, which has a regular rhythmic, rhyming pattern. Notice the rhyme and rhythm in the first three stanzas of the poem.

> Listen, my children, and you shall hear
> Of the midnight ride of Paul Revere,
> On the eighteenth of April, in Seventy-five:
> Hardly a man is now alive
> Who remembers that famous day and year.
>
> He said to his friend, "If the British march
> By land or sea from the town to-night,
> Hang a lantern aloft in the belfry arch
> Of the North Church tower as a signal light,—
> One, if by land, and two, if by sea;
> And I on the opposite shore will be,
> Ready to ride and spread the alarm
> Through every Middlesex village and farm,
> For the country folk to be up and to arm."
>
> Then he said, "Good night!" and with muffled oar
> Silently rowed to the Charlestown shore,
> Just as the moon rose over the bay,
> Where swinging wide at her moorings lay
> The Somerset, British man-of-war;
> A phantom ship, with each mast and spar
> Across the moon like a prison bar,
> And a huge black hulk, that was magnified
> By its own reflection in the tide.

HENRY WADSWORTH LONGFELLOW (1807–1882)

Free Verse In contrast to traditional poetry, **free verse** does not have a regular rhyme or rhythm pattern and is frequently used by writers today. Below, Walt Whitman's poem titled "I Saw in Louisiana a Live-Oak Growing" is an example of free verse.

> I saw in Louisiana a live-oak growing,
> All alone stood it, and the moss hung down from the
>   branches;
> Without any companion it grew there, uttering joyous
>   leaves of dark green,
> And its look, rude, unbending, lusty, made me think
>   of myself;
> But I wonder'd how it could utter joyous leaves,
>   standing alone there, without its friend, its lover
>   near—for I knew I could not;
> And broke off a twig with a certain number of leaves
>   upon it, and twined around it a little moss,
> And brought it away—and I have placed it in sight
>   in my room;
> It is not needed to remind me as of my own dear friends,
> (For I believe lately I think of little else than them,)
> Yet it remains to me a curious token—it makes me think
>   of manly love;
> For all that, and though the live-oak glistens there in
>   Louisiana, solitary, in a wide flat space,
> Uttering joyous leaves all its life, without a friend, a
>   lover, near,
> I know very well I could not.

WALT WHITMAN (1819–1892)

Although the free verse above does not contain rhyme or regular rhythm, it is full of clear, sharp images. Notice how the author gives human qualities to the tree: "uttering joyous leaves of dark green…without its friend, its lover, near."

Selecting a Subject In selecting a subject for a poem, make a list of things about which you feel strongly. Using the lines provided, write your ideas for each of the following:

• an important person in your life

_____

• a place you remember with strong emotion

_____

- an activity that you love or hate

_____

- your most or least favorite season or time of day

_____

- your most or least favorite holiday

_____

- a meaningful experience or observation

_____

- a possession that you value

_____

- music that you enjoy or dislike

_____

- your most or least favorite animal

_____

- your most or least favorite food

_____

- an object that you appreciate or despise

_____

After writing one or more ideas under each category above, think about why you feel strongly about each item. Then circle three that you would consider using as the subject of a poem.

Gathering Thoughts about your Subject

Using a separate sheet of paper, brainstorm about at least one of your three possible subjects circled above, as in the following example:

Uncle Bob's big backyard

fragrant pink and red roses
volleyball games with cousins
huge, spreading oak tree
cooling off in swimming pool
aroma of citrus blossoms
birthday parties
Uncle Bob playing harmonica
Aunt Christie on accordion
the lazy hammock
exploring the tool shed

skunks and possums
barbecued hamburgers
picking peaches and plums
lizards and spiders
romping with the dog

After brainstorming, place a check mark beside the ideas that most clearly express your feelings. Copy those onto another sheet of paper leaving plenty of space between each one for more details. Then write as many specific details as you can to fully describe each expression, as in the following example:

√ the lazy hammock
    wind rushing through willow trees sounds like running water
    strong, weathered rope mesh supports my weary body
    gently rocking in cool shade and fresh air
    a quiet place away from TV, homework, people, distractions
    a place to rest, to listen, to think, and to dream
    doves coo nearby
    horns honk in the distance

Practice

Complete the steps given in this lesson for selecting a subject and gathering thoughts for your own poem. Save your notes in your folder or binder so that you can add to them at any time. You will use these notes for writing poems in the next two lessons.

Writing a Traditional Poem

We have learned that a traditional poem has regular rhythm and rhyme. In this lesson, we shall discuss a few different ways to create rhythm and rhyme in a traditional poem.

Rhythm   Rhythm is the regular repetition or orderly recurrence of sounds or accented syllables. To create rhythm, we combine words to take advantage of their natural accents. Notice the alternating stressed (´) and unstressed (˘) syllables in the following lines:

> Moun̆tain/ tall an̆d/ ocean/ deep
> Trembling/ balan̆ce/ duly/ keep.
>
> RALPH WALDO EMERSON ("COMPENSATION")
>
> It was/ the schoo/ner Hes/perus
> That sailed/ the win/tery sea.
>
> HENRY WADSWORTH LONGFELLOW

While most traditional poetry has a regular rhythmic pattern, this pattern may not be the same in every line. It may change from one line to another, remaining consistent within the whole poem, as in the example below. Notice that the first and third lines each have five accented syllables or words while the second and fourth lines each have only three.

> Not/ gold,/ but on/ly man/ can make
> A peo/ple great/ and strong.
> Men/ who/ for truth/ and hon/or's sake
> Stand fast/ and suf/fer long.
>
> RALPH WALDO EMERSON

Rhyme   In addition to rhythmic patterns, we can create rhyming patterns to enhance our poetry. Patterns of repeated sounds may be regular or random. They may occur at the beginning, middle, or end of lines. Traditional poetry contains regular rhyme as well as regular rhythm. In Ralph Waldo Emerson's poem above, the last word in every other line of the stanza (a grouping of lines in a poem) rhymes. However, Christina

Rossetti's poem below is written in couplets, two successive rhyming lines that form a unit:

A Dirge

Why were you born when the snow was falling?
You should have come to the cuckoo's calling
Or when grapes are green in the cluster,
Or, at least, when lithe swallows muster
    For their far off flying
    From summer dying.

Why did you die when the lambs were cropping?
You should have died at the apples' dropping,
When the grasshopper comes to trouble,
And the wheat-fields are sodden stubble,
    And all winds go sighing
    For sweet things dying.

Another common rhyming pattern is the limerick, which is often used in humorous poetry and follows an AABBA rhyme scheme, meaning that each limerick is made up of two couplets plus a fifth line that rhymes with the first two, as in the examples below:

[A]   There was an old man of Calcutta,
[A]   Who coated his tonsils with butta,
[B]   Thus converting his snore
[B]   From a thunderous roar
[A]   To a soft, oleaginous mutta.

OGDEN NASH

[A]   A flea and a fly in a flue
[A]   Were imprisoned, so what could they do?
[B]   Said the fly, "Let us flee!"
[B]   "Let us fly!" said the flea.
[A]   So they flew through a flaw in the flue.

OGDEN NASH

Practice   Using some of the ideas you developed in the previous lesson, write a traditional poem of at least four lines with regular rhyme and rhythm. Try to rhyme important words with words that support the meaning of your poem. Be mindful of stressed and unstressed syllables as you create a rhythm with your words.

LESSON 32

Writing a Free-verse Poem

We have learned that free verse does not have regular rhyme or rhythm. In free verse, repeated sounds are more likely to be irregular and inexact, like the sounds of speech. Sensory details and vivid language create clear images and strong messages. In this lesson, we shall use all we have learned about descriptive writing and poetry to create our own free-verse poem.

Repeated Sounds

In free verse, repeated sounds may occur at the beginning, middle, or end of lines. They may be in the form of *assonance*, the repetition of a particular vowel sound; *consonance*, the repetition of a particular consonant sound within or at the end of words; or *alliteration*, the repetition of identical or similar sounds at the beginning of words.

ASSONANCE: giddy Nick is kissing fish

CONSONANCE: Tommy's mama hums and hammers

ALLITERATION: frying fish for Friday's feast

In addition to the types of repeated sounds above, free verse may employ rhyming words, but they are not confined to a certain pattern as in traditional poetry. For example, a line of free verse might include these words: coat/throat/note/wrote

Figurative Language

In writing free verse, poets also use figurative language, or *figures of speech*, which include the simile, the metaphor, and the personification. We have learned to create vivid descriptions using sensory detail and comparisons such as similes and metaphors. We remember that the simile expresses similarity between two things by using the word *like* or *as*:

And who can stand when He appears?
For He is *like a refiner's fire*
And *like launderers' soap.*
MALACHI 3:2, NEW KING JAMES VERSION

All we *like sheep* have gone astray.
ISAIAH 53:6, NEW KING JAMES VERSION

You shall come to the grave at a full age, *as a sheaf of grain ripens in its season.* JOB 5:26, NEW KING JAMES VERSION

With favor You will surround him *as with a shield.*
PSALM 5:12, NEW KING JAMES VERSION

The metaphor, on the other hand, describes one thing as though it were another thing:

Their throat *is an open tomb.*

PSALM 5:9, NEW KING JAMES VERSION

The Lord *is my rock and my fortress.*

PSALM 18:2, NEW KING JAMES VERSION

Another form of figurative language is *personification*, a metaphor in which human qualities are given to nonliving things, abstract ideas, or animals. Notice how mountains, hills, and trees are personified in the following metaphors:

For you shall go out with joy,
And be led out with peace;
The mountains and the hills
Shall break forth into singing before you,
And all the trees of the field shall clap their hands.

ISAIAH 55:12, NEW KING JAMES VERSION

Beneath some patriarchal tree
I lay upon the ground;
His hoary arms uplifted he,
And all the broad leaves over me
Clapped their little hands in glee,
With one continuous sound:—

FROM HENRY WADSWORTH LONGFELLOW'S "PRELUDE"

Simile, metaphor, and personification will enhance your free verse.

Practice Using the ideas you developed in Lesson 30, or some new ideas, write a free-verse poem of at least eight lines. Concentrate on important words that express your ideas, and put them in a meaningful order. Try to create clear, vivid images using sensory details—sights, sounds, smells, and other physical sensations. In addition, you might use simile, metaphor, or personification as well as repeated sounds.

Avoiding Plagiarism

What is Plagiarism? We have learned that failing to give an author credit for his or her ideas is called **plagiarism.** We know that plagiarism is against the law, for it is intellectual theft, an act which is just as unacceptable as material theft. For this reason, people who *plagiarize,* or steal other people's ideas, find themselves in serious trouble. Therefore, we must carefully give credit to authors and sources that we use in our essays and research papers.

Whenever we use ideas from a source, we must give credit to that source, whether we quote exactly from an author or use our own words. Sometimes students incorrectly believe that paraphrasing facts and ideas from a source removes the problem of plagiarism. This is not so. If the information is not original with you, then you must footnote it even if you have used your own words, or paraphrased the information.

Any fact, data, language, or idea that did not come from your own mind needs to be footnoted unless it is *common knowledge.*

What is Common Knowledge? **Common knowledge** is information that most people know. For example, most people know that George Washington was the first President of the United States and that the Constitution of the United States was signed in 1787. These facts are common knowledge and do not require footnotes.

On the other hand, if the fact is something that most people would *not* know, then it needs a footnote. For example, not everyone knows when Abraham Lincoln married Mary Todd, and not many people know the birth dates of John Adams's children. These facts are not common knowledge, so they would require footnotes.

If you are uncertain as to whether specific information is common knowledge or whether it needs a footnote, ask your teacher.

In this lesson, we shall practice determining what information needs a footnote and what does not.

Example Carol Walworth's "Autobiography" begins like this:

> World War II ended in 1945, and I was born three years later. Many babies were born in our country right after the war, and I was one of them. Yes, I am a part of the "baby boom" generation.

We find the following pieces of information in Carol Walworth's "Autobiography." Mark each one to indicate whether it is common knowledge (no footnote necessary) or information that needs a footnote. For a–d, circle "footnote" or "no footnote."

(a) The year 1945 marked the end of World War II. (footnote, no footnote)

(b) Carol Walworth was born in 1948. (footnote, no footnote)

(c) In the years following World War II, many babies were born in the United States. (footnote, no footnote)

(d) Carol Walworth is a part of the "baby boom" generation. (footnote, no footnote)

Solution We consider whether or not the information is common knowledge. If it is common knowledge, we circle "no footnote." But if the information is not common knowledge, we circle "footnote."

(a) The year 1946 marked the end of World War II. (footnote, (no footnote)) This information is common knowledge.

(b) Carol Walworth was born in 1948. ((footnote), no footnote) Not many people know Carol Walworth or her birth date.

(c) In the years following World War II, many babies were born in the United States. (footnote, (no footnote)) Most people know that the war was followed by a large population increase in the United States.

(d) Carol Walworth is a part of the "baby boom" generation. ((footnote), no footnote) Carol Walworth is one of a multitude of "baby boomers," and she is not famous, so this is not common knowledge and must be footnoted.

Practice An entry from Chase Blackbeard's bird journal titled "Hit the Road" begins as follows:

> Since many birds migrate south for the winter, I decided to follow them. On October 3, 2004, I packed up my binoculars and my digital camera and left Brick, New Jersey. I headed south toward Central America, where many birds spend the winter. There I hoped to observe and photograph the American redstart and the rose-breasted grosbeak during mating season, which is when they are the most colorful.

We find the following pieces of information in Chase Blackbeard's journal. Mark each one to indicate whether it is common knowledge (no footnote necessary) or information that needs a footnote. For a–e, circle "footnote" or "no footnote."

a. Some birds that live in New Jersey migrate south for the winter. (footnote, no footnote)

b. Chase Blackbeard decided to follow the birds that were flying south. (footnote, no footnote)

c. Many species of birds spend the winter in Central America. (footnote, no footnote)

d. With his digital camera, Chase Blackbeard wants to photograph the American redstart and the rose-breasted grosbeak. (footnote, no footnote)

e. Birds are the most colorful during mating season. (footnote, no footnote)

Circle the simple subject and underline the simple predicate in each sentence. If the subject is understood, write "(you)" after the sentence.

1. Is exercise beneficial?

2. Join me at the park for some exercise.

3. Chase Blakely runs four miles each day.

4. His beagle goes with him.

5. They circle the park twice at six-minutes per mile pace.

6. Have you seen them?

7. Yesterday, Chase's beagle disappeared.

8. Perhaps the dog is lost!

9. Keep your eyes open for him.

10. Is Chase's dog swimming in the lake?

11. Has he wandered into the city streets?

12. Chase has been searching for him all morning.

13. Will you help Chase and me?

14. Today, there are no dogs in sight.

15. A jogger in a baseball cap saw a beagle near the highway.

16. The beagle near the highway was barking at the jogger.

17. Can you imagine Chase's anguish over his lost dog?

18. Will Chase's dog find his way home?

19. Has he been stolen by a dognapper?

20. Here comes Chase's beagle!

Circle each letter that should be capitalized in these sentences.

1. the eastern hemisphere has four continents: europe, asia, africa, and australia.

2. the western hemisphere has two continents, north america and south america.

3. the seventh continent, antarctica, is at the southern tip of both hemispheres.

4. did mr. andrew angles cross the atlantic ocean on a ship called queen mary?

5. my friend miss farris teaches english and spanish at arroyo high school in el monte, california.

6. many years ago, grandpa curtis hiked mount whitney.

7. on wednesday, uncle bill will go fishing in peck park lake.

8. next october the sanchez family will cruise the st. lawrence river.

9. did a shot at fort sumter start the civil war?

10. the first major man-made canal in the united states was the erie canal, which connected lake erie with the hudson river.

11. from the top of mount wilson, i could see catalina island off the coast of california.

12. on tuesday, mr. yu flew from los angeles international airport to his home in newark, new jersey.

13. from the plane he saw the mojave desert, the sierra nevada mountains, the mississippi river, and the statue of liberty.

14. sir cumference, a member of the british parliament, wanted to sail around the world but made it only as far as iceland.

More Practice Lesson 6

Underline the entire verb phrase in each sentence.

1. Mark Twain <u>was born</u> in the town of Florida, Missouri, on November 30, 1835.

2. His family <u>had moved</u> there from Tennessee.

3. Twain <u>must have had</u> a happy childhood in Hannibal, Missouri.

4. He <u>may have watched</u> the steamboats on the Mississippi River.

5. <u>Did</u> he <u>explore</u> the great forests as a child?

6. <u>Had</u> his father <u>been</u> a successful lawyer?

7. His mother <u>might have encouraged</u> his sense of humor.

8. For four years, Mark Twain <u>was piloting</u> riverboats on the Mississippi.

9. He <u>must have become</u> familiar with all the towns along the river.

10. <u>Shall</u> we <u>read</u> his first short story, "The Celebrated Jumping Frog of Calaveras County"?

11. <u>Can</u> you <u>imagine</u> life on the Mississippi in those days?

12. <u>Would</u> you <u>have befriended</u> Huck Finn?

13. <u>Does</u> Tom Sawyer's life <u>appeal</u> to you?

14. <u>Could</u> you <u>have lived</u> with the Widow Douglas and her sister, Miss Watson?

15. Judge Thatcher <u>had invested</u> money for Huck.

16. Dressed as a girl, Huck <u>will visit</u> Mrs. Loftus.

17. Peter Wilks <u>has</u> recently <u>died</u>.

18. Dr. Robinson and Levi Bell <u>have recognized</u> the guise of the duke and the king.

Hysterical Fiction #1

An Election

Follows Lesson 8

Teacher instructions: Have students number blank, lined papers from 1 to 27. Ask them to write an example of the indicated part of speech beside each number. Proceed slowly, and be sure each student has written a correct example of the part of speech you have requested for each blank space in the story.
Next, give students a copy of the story, and ask them to write each word from their list into the blanks with the corresponding numbers.
Finally, ask students to read their stories aloud.

(1) _____ and (2) _____ formed a
proper noun (person)   proper noun (person)

committee to elect Ms. Bogus to serve on the local school

board in (3) _____. They first took time to
proper noun (place)

(4)_____ and (5) _____. Then, with
present tense action verb   present tense action verb

purpose and zeal, they embarked on a strategy to defeat Ms.

Bogus's opponents, (6) _____ and
proper noun (person)

(7)_____. To advertize Ms. Bogus's worthy qualities,
proper noun (person)

the committee designed posters showing her with her

(8)_____ and her beloved (9) _____. The
concrete plural noun   masculine noun

poster text read, "The well-educated Ms. Bogus has studied

(10) _____. She will protect your
abstract proper noun

(11)_____. She will demand
concrete plural noun

(12)_____and (13) _____ in schools."
abstract common noun   abstract common noun

To attract public attention, the committee

(14)_____ and (15) _____ in the streets
past tense action verb   past tense action verb

as they passed out flyers to every (16) _____ and
masculine singular noun

(17) _____ they saw.
feminine singular noun

Unfortunately, Ms. Bogus's opponents recruited a

(18)_____ of (19) _____ to ridicule and
collective noun   masculine plural noun

smear her in an online campaign by revealing her secret stash

of (20) _____. Fortunately, they were not aware of
concrete plural noun

her (21) _____ collection or of her former alliance
concrete singular noun

with (22) _____ in (23) _____.
proper noun (person)   proper noun (person)

Will Ms. Bogus have the (24) _____ to win?
abstract common noun

Circle each letter that should be capitalized in these sentences.

1. we remember sir thomas More for his literary work *utopia* which describes an imaginary ideal society.

2. abraham lincoln said, "truth is generally the best vindication against slander."

3. have you read the poem "paul revere's ride" by henry wadsworth longfellow?

4. ralph waldo emerson wrote, "it is better to suffer injustice than to do it."

5. geoffrey chaucer's *the canterbury tales* shows the life of fourteenth century english society.

6. henry ward beecher once said, "it is not work that kills men; it is worry."

7. in *the book of martyrs*, john foxe wrote about martyrs of the christian church.

8. robert leighton said, "god's choice acquaintances are humble [people]."

9. in the late 1500s, edmund spenser wrote his masterpiece, *the faerie queen*, an allegorical, epic romance.

10. curious, benito asked, "why did delilah cut samson's hair?

11. president dwight d. eisenhower said, "the spirit of man is more important than mere physical strength, and the spiritual fiber of a nation than its wealth."

12. a puritan named john trapp once said, "conscience is god's spy and man's overseer."

13. like spenser's *faerie queen*, john bunyan's *pilgrim's progress* is an allegory, a narrative in which the characters and places are symbols.

14. i. electric energy
    a. charge
    b. circuits

    ii. radiant energy
    a. light
    b. colors

15. in the book of *hebrews*, god promises, "i will never leave you, nor forsake you."

Circle each letter that should be capitalized in these sentences.

1. does bea helty sneak green beans into her peach pies?

2. last spring, i took professor cuilty's social studies class.

3. did miss blom teach spanish at stanford university?

4. do grandma and grandpa otto speak german?

5. on sunday, father o'rourke will officiate in latin at holy angels catholic church in loveland, colorado.

6. will dad meet aunt margaret for lunch?

7. at the hospital, rabbi feingold read to several patients from the torah.

8. under his arm, wassim carried a well-used copy of the koran, islam's holy book.

9. yes, i believe dr. dinwitty works at huntington memorial hospital.

10. has captain rice returned from the u. s. air force?

11. after a twelve-month tour of duty, sergeant lopez will return from saudi arabia.

12. he has written frequently to his father in texas.

13. in her distress, saryati called upon allah, the arabic term for god.

14. in august, uncle jasper flew from newark, new jersey, to honolulu, hawaii.

15. yesterday, mieko reminisced about her years in a japanese internment camp in california during world war ii.

16. can you tell the difference between a beagle and a russian wolfhound?

Hysterical Fiction #2

A Letter to Congress

Follows Lesson 23

Having learned much about (1) _____ and
_____
abstract proper noun

(2)_____ in school, (3) _____ decided to
_____   _____
abstract proper noun   proper noun (person)

write the following letter to Congress to set the nation straight

on certain issues:

Dear Congressperson,

I and my friend (4) _____ have noticed a dismal
_____
proper noun (person)

lack of (5) _____ and (6) _____ in our
_____   _____
abstract common noun   concrete common noun

country. We have been (7)_____ and
_____
pres. participle form of verb

(8)_____ in order to rectify the situation, but we
_____
pres. participle form of verb

need your help. Lawless people have (9)_____ and
_____
past participle form of verb

(10)_____. They threaten to destroy the
_____
past participle form of verb

(11)_____ (12)_____ and replace them
_____   _____
descriptive adjective   concrete plural noun

with (13)_____ (14)_____. We cannot let
_____   _____
descriptive adjective   concrete plural noun

this happen. If necessary, we (15)_____
_____
1st person future tense verb

(16)_____ (17)_____, and we
_____   _____
preposition   concrete plural noun

(18)_____ (19)_____
_____   _____
1st person future tense verb   preposition

(20)_____ to prove our point. No one is
_____
abstract singular noun

(21)_____ (22)_____, or
_____   _____
preposition   preposition

(23)_____ the law of our land.
_____
preposition

Sincerely yours,

Two (24)_____ and (25)_____ citizens
_____   _____
descriptive adjective   descriptive adjective

Underline each adjective in these sentences.

1. Three main climate zones include the frigid zone, the temperate zone, and the torrid zone.

2. The polar climate of the frigid zone causes a frozen ice cap throughout the entire year.

3. In the tundra climate of this frigid zone, some plants will grow, but no trees will grow.

4. The taiga climate of the temperate zone allows for vast forests of conifer trees.

5. The marine climate has moderate temperatures and much rain and is found on west coasts of some continents.

6. The continental steppe is a treeless plain with cold winters, hot summers, and little rainfall.

7. In the interiors of some continents, we find the humid continental climate with hot summers, cold winters, and much rainfall.

8. The humid subtropic climate has hot, moist summers, mild winters, thick forests, and dense populations.

9. This climate is found on east coasts of continents.

10. The subtropical desert, on the other hand, produces hot, dry summers and cold, dry winters.

11. The Mediterranean climate has a mild, rainy winter and a hot, dry summer.

12. Luscious citrus fruits, olive trees, and cedar trees grow in this type of temperate zone.

13. The tropical rain forest in the torrid zone is known for its scorching heat, humid atmosphere, tall trees, and heavy vines.

14. Many interesting animals live in the savanna where tall, tough grasses and some trees grow.

15. Mr. Haroon's safari took him to remote places.

16. Few people have visited these regions.

17. His jeep lost its brakes as it thundered down a steep, bumpy road.

18. Several swift gnus with curved horns came to the rescue.

Circle each letter that should be capitalized in these sentences.

1. if i'm not mistaken, lieutenant peabody is now stationed in the northwest.

2. mr. and mrs. chen attend bethlehem lutheran church on halifax street.

3. next saturday, miss campos will read "the cat in the hat" to children at the alhambra public library.

4. baptists, methodists, and catholics worship jesus christ as god's son.

5. onping yu, a buddhist monk, often travels to the far east.

6. people came to america to worship in their own way.

7. how did moses and the hebrew people cross the red sea?

8. james studied the natural history of a southwest area called death valley.

9. dr. martin luther king, jr. challenged people from all over the country, but especially from the south.

10. as world war ii was ending, ruth gruber helped thousands of jewish refugees to escape nazi terror and make their homes in our country.

11. dear ms. werk,
    i could not attend english class yesterday because i was sick.
    > regretfully,
    > tony

12. dear tony,
    you are excused from class. i hope you feel better.
    > sincerely,
    > ms. werk

13. dear ms. werk,
    dr. bandage says i must remain at home until friday.
    > regretfully,
    > tony

Circle every capital letter that does not belong in these sentences.

1. In his Physical Education class, Michael played Water Polo and Football.

2. At the Zoo, I saw an African Rhinoceros and a Hippopotamus.

3. In addition to English Walnuts, Colonel Mustard grows Pecans and Washington Apples.

4. His wife has planted Pansies, Marigolds, and African Violets.

5. Would you like French Vanilla or Dutch Chocolate Ice Cream?

6. Until she caught the German measles, Lana was enrolled in Geometry, Biology, and Astronomy.

7. Beth likes Tamales and Enchiladas, but Freddy prefers Chinese Food.

8. Next Spring, we will plant Cucumbers, Green Beans, and Italian Squash.

9. Our Apricots, Peaches, and Plums ripen in early Summer.

10. In the Fall, our Friends, the Lopezes, will move to the South.

11. During the Winter, the Black Squirrels burrow under the snow.

12. I believe Mr. Zee is recovering from a bad case of Conjunctivitis that he caught from his Gnu.

13. Last Summer, he suffered from Gastroenteritis after eating too much New York Cheese Cake.

14. He has been playing Hide-And-Seek and Ping Pong for entertainment.

15. My Mom made Swiss Cheese sandwiches for lunch and Chocolate Eclairs for dessert.

16. Elspeth found a Japanese Beetle in her Chicken Casserole.

Use the standard proofreading symbols to correct the errors in each writing sample.

1. Dear Mr Groovey,

   thankyou for taking care of My chickens while I was in japan on Tuesday, Wendsday, and Thursday I'm sorry they pecked wholes in your car cover. Wasn't that funny?

   your neighbor,

   Sam

2. Dear Sam,

   i didnot find it humorous that your chickens ripped holes in the cover for my new car. Worse yet, thay nearly drowned my swimming pool as they tried to drink the the water. Nevertheless, i shall take the blame for thees mishaps since I Had for gotten to give the chickens food or water that day.

   sincerely,

   Harold Groovey

3. mr Hake will eat green beans, lima beans, adn pintobeans; but he he prefers jelly beans.

4. Have you ever misplaced some thing inportant to you One morning, Christie could not find her iron for Pressing her clothes.

5. Later, she foundit beside a Carton of milk when she opened the refrijerator!

6. While in the hospital, Uncle lionel had a brain scan. Just as I thought, Dr Dimwitty couldnot find any thing

7. Uncle Lionel sold all his appliances when heMoved to to kansas Un fortunately, he'd left his false teeeth in the the dishwashre!

Diagram each sentence.

1. Wilbur and Orville created wonderful kites and mechanical toys.

2. The brothers rented, sold, and built bicycles.

3. They continued to dream and to experiment.

4. Bird-watching gave Orville and Wilbur new ideas.

5. The Wright Brothers, tireless and determined, patented an airplane.

Place commas where they are needed in these sentences.

1. By 1775 a huge rift had developed between the American colonies and England.

2. John Hancock was elected president of the Second Continental Congress on May 10 1775 the day Fort Ticonderoga fell.

3. On June 17 1775 the British engaged the Patriots at the Battle of Bunker Hill.

4. On July 6 1775 the Second Continental Congress adopted a *Declaration of the Causes and Necessity of Taking Up Arms.*

5. George III issued a *Proclamation of Rebellion* on August 23 1775 declaring that Americans were in open rebellion.

6. Paul Revere William Dawes and Dr. Samuel Prescott worked together to warn the colonists that the British soldiers were coming to Lexington Massachusetts.

7. By March of 1776 the Americans had taken the city of Boston Massachusetts.

8. On July 4 1776 the Continental Congress unanimously adopted the *Declaration of Independence.*

9. The *Declaration of Independence* affirms the rights of all people to life liberty and the pursuit of happiness.

10. In Philadelphia Pennsylvania you can see Independence Hall as well as the Liberty Bell.

For 11–14, place commas where they are needed in these addresses.

11. 11147 Bunbury Street Saint Louis Missouri

12. 270 Alta Vista Drive Tallahassee Florida

13. 4921 Cedar Avenue Topeka Kansas

14. 30 Pine Street Denver Colorado

Place commas where they are needed in these sentences.

1. Harvey please pass the mashed potatoes.

2. Maristela Ilbea's sister coaches cross country at the high school.

3. Penny Kurt's lively beagle leaps six-foot fences.

4. Did you feed the dog Molly?

5. I hope Mauricio that you locked your python's cage.

6. Allison Curtis R.N. treated hundreds of patients in Mexico last month.

7. Has Dolores Dolorfino M.D. diagnosed your ailment yet?

8. May we paint your apartment for you Mr. Rivas?

9. Richard M. Curtis D.D.S. will straighten those crooked teeth.

10. I think Miss Vong Treasurer conducted the meeting in October.

11. Salvador Placencia pastor of Yardly Friends Church opened the meeting with prayer.

12. Did Sergio Cabrera Ph.D. speak at your graduation ceremony?

13. The famous Pac Couch District Attorney won another case in court today.

14. We will eat lunch at the Peacock Cafe my favorite restaurant.

15. Our school's vice principal Mrs. Margie Kierstein suggested that we plant seven new evergreen trees.

16. I hope dear friend that you recover quickly.

17. Jumana Musulli a noteable theologian discussed the Dead Sea Scrolls.

18. The youngest city council candidate Isael Hermosillo has an excellent chance of winning.

Hysterical Fiction #3

A Preservation Society

Follows Lesson 44

Concerned about the depletion of the (1)_____,
                                                                      concrete plural noun

the   (2)_____,   and   the   (3)_____   in
                   abstract singular noun   concrete plural noun

(4)_____,   (5)_____,   (6)_____,
         proper noun (place)   proper noun (person)   proper noun (person)

and (7)_____ formed a preservation society.
             proper noun (person)

(8)_____   and   (9)_____,
         pres. participle form of verb   pres. participle form of verb

(10)_____   (11)_____,   and
           preposition   preposition

(12)_____   their   first   meeting,   the
           preposition

(13)_____   society   members   vowed   to
        number adjective

(14)_____ all (15)_____. They pledged
     pres. tense transitive verb   abstract singular noun

their   allegiance   to   each   other   and   to   all   the

(16)_____   (17)_____   everywhere.   To
      superlative adjective   feminine plural noun

create   public   awareness   of   the   problem,   they

(18)_____   (19)_____
     past tense transitive verb   masculine plural noun

(20)_____   (21)_____   zealously.   They
   coordinating conjunction   past tense intransitive action verb

also   designed   t-shirts   and   bumper   stickers   picturing   a

(22)_____   of   (23)_____   and
        collective noun   concrete plural noun

(24)_____   (25)_____   to   stir
     descriptive adjective   concrete plural noun

(26)_____ within the hearts of all people.
      abstract singular noun

Although (27)_____ aided their efforts, most
                      proper noun (person)

(28)_____ opposed them. In the end, the society
      feminine plural noun

proved (29)_____ than their opponent.
              comparative adjective

Place commas where they are needed.

1. Dear Trevor
   Please walk the dog.
          Love
          Jared

2. My dear brother
   I couldn't find Rex.
          Sorry
          Trevor

3. Dear Cousin
   I'll see you at the train station next Saturday!
          Yours truly
          Justin

4. The index listed "Washington George" on page 447.

5. She wrote "Hake Danielle" since the application requested last name first.

6. Jonathan Edwards and George Whitefield both dynamic preachers sparked the Great Awakening in Colonial America.

7. In fact this religious movement encouraged the creation of new institutions of higher learning.

8. Princeton University for example grew out of the early revivalist William Tennent's Log College.

9. In addition the Anglican King's College became Columbia University.

10. The Baptists I understand established what is now Brown University.

11. Furthermore the Congregationalists established Dartmouth College in 1769.

12. On numerous trips to the colonies George Whitefield preached about the need for each individual to experience a "new birth."

13. Renowned for his "fire and brimstone" sermons Jonathan Edwards warned sinners about the fate of those who would not repent.

14. "New Lights" supporters of the revival split from the "Old Lights" those who opposed the revival.

15. At the same time the Great Awakening minimized differences between Protestant denominations.

16. Moreover church membership increased greatly along with the creation of new churches.

Underline the dependent clause in each sentence, and circle the subordinating conjunction.

1. We remember that General Thomas Gage served as the military Governor of Massachusetts.

2. As General Thomas Gage fortified Boston in the fall of 1774, the colonists prepared small militias called Minute Men.

3. Although the groups of Minute Men were small, they were armed and ready for quick action.

4. If the British army approached, William Dawes and Paul Revere would ride out to alert the local townspeople and farmers.

5. The British continued on to Concord after they left Lexington.

6. The British won the Battle of Bunker Hill even though they lost a thousand men.

7. Ethan Allen led the Green Mountain Boys of Vermont to capture Fort Ticonderoga while Boston was being besieged.

8. The Second Continental Congress met in Philadelphia as fighting raged.

9. Even though the colonists were already fighting against British, the Second Continental Congress adopted the Olive Branch Petition, professing loyalty to the Crown.

10. While the colonists were battling for their rights, they desired peace with the British.

11. The Continental Congress assumed governmental responsibilities when the British refused to cooperate.

12. When the troops around Boston were declared a Continental Army, George Washington was named its commander.

13. The Continental Congress created a navy and sought allies in Europe since George III had rejected the Olive Branch Petition.

14. Parliament closed the colonies to all trade as soon as George III rejected the Olive Branch Petition.

For 1–6, underline each participial phrase and circle the word it modifies.

1. The pilgrim, strengthened by adversity, kept the faith.

2. Having stated her objections, Isabel stood firm.

3. That miner leading the mule is my uncle.

4. Jogging along the levee, Ms. Rivas saw some hedgehogs.

5. Having lost his keys, Nigel could not start his car.

6. The little girl building sand castles is my niece.

For 7–10, complete the diagram of each sentence.

7. Your worrying will accomplish nothing.

8. Julita enjoys trimming her trees.

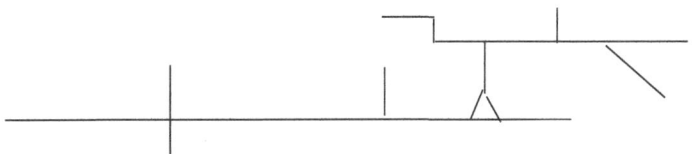

9. Supporting the British, Loyalists fought the Patriots.

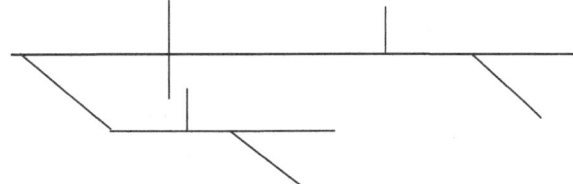

10. Having painted the entire house, Jenny relaxed.

Place commas where they are needed in these sentences.

1. British troops were well armed supplied and trained.

2. Although the British had a professional army communication with commanders across the ocean sometimes broke down.

3. As the cost of war rose taxes rose also in Great Britain.

4. Since Britain had the largest navy in the world the Patriots faced a formidable foe.

5. Though George Washington had limited military experience he managed to lead the poorly trained undisciplined militia.

6. George Washington's army often lacked food medicine and ammunition.

7. Because the Continental Congress had no power to tax the colonies or raise an army the Continental Army suffered.

8. Though the British troops had many advantages they were not fighting on their own soil.

9. When Americans read Thomas Paine's *Common Sense* their attitudes changed toward George III.

10. In June of 1776 a committee appointed by the Continental Congress began drafting a declaration of independence.

11. The committee members included Thomas Jefferson John Adams and Benjamin Franklin.

12. Since about twenty-one thousand Loyalists fought with the British the American Revolution seemed like a civil war.

13. Loyalists Native Americans and slaves sided with the British.

14. Although the Second Continental Congress grew increasingly powerful they did not declare independence until more than a year after fighting had begun.

Place commas where they are needed in these sentences.

1. The undisciplined Patriots had to mature or they would lose the war.

2. George Washington would not surrender nor would he abandon the cause.

3. Determination strengthens resolve but vacillation can bring disaster.

4. The Continental Army survived their harsh winter encampments at Valley Forge for they had faith.

5. The Patriots needed support from other nations so they looked to France.

6. The Patriots were defeated on Long Island and Manhattan yet they were victorious at Trenton and Princeton.

7. The war was over for Cornwallis had laid down his arms.

8. Benjamin Franklin said "Content makes poor men rich; discontent makes rich men poor."

9. In *Othello,* William Shakespeare wrote "Poor and content is rich and rich enough."

10. "The noblest mind the best contentment has" wrote Edmund Spencer in *The Faerie Queen.*

11. "To know what is right and not do it is the worst cowardice" said Confucius.

12. An old French proverb says "Justifying a fault doubles it."

13. Woodrow Wilson said "I believe in democracy because it releases the energies of every human being."

14. On December 14, 1799, George Washington spoke his last words "Doctor, I die hard, but I am not afraid to go."

15. On his deathbed in 1848, John Quincy Adams said "This is the last of earth! I am content."

16. Referring to the American flag, Charles Sumner said "White is for purity, red for valor, blue for justice."

Place quotation marks where they are needed in these sentences.

1. Oliver Wendell Holmes said, Fame usually comes to those who are thinking about something else.

2. They are able because they think they are able, said Virgil in *Aeneid*.

3. A Hindu proverb warns, Even nectar is poison if taken in excess.

4. It is better to be the enemy of a wise man, said the Hindu sage, than the friend of a fool.

5. A wise man will make haste to forgive, said Samuel Johnson, because he knows the true value of time, and will not suffer it to pass away in unnecessary pain.

6. A Danish proverb says, There is no need to hang a bell on a fool.

7. Dig a well before you are thirsty, advised the Chinese scholar.

8. Life has taught me to forgive, said Otto von Bismarck, but to seek forgiveness still more.

9. Free countries are those in which the rights of man are respected, said Robespierre, and the laws, in consequence, are just.

10. Those who deny freedom to others deserve it not for themselves, said Lincoln, and, under a just God, cannot long retain it.

11. Rudyard Kipling said, All we have of freedom—all we use or know—This our fathers bought for us, long and long ago.

12. Freedom exists, said Woodrow Wilson, only where people take care of the government.

13. Leonardo da Vinci advised, Reprove a friend in secret, but praise him before others.

14. A friend should bear his friend's infirmities, wrote Shakespeare.

For 1-16, place quotation marks where they are needed in the dialogs.

We read this dialogue in *The Scarlet Letter* by Nathaniel Hawthorne:

1.   Child, what art thou? cried the mother.

2.   Oh, I am your little Pearl! answered the child.

3.   Art thou my child, in very truth? asked Hester.

4.   Yes; I am little Pearl! repeated the child, continuing her antics.

We find this dialogue in *Kim* by Rudyard Kipling:

5.   What is this? said the boy, standing before him. Hast thou been robbed?.

6.   It is my new *chela* (my disciple) that is gone away from me, and I know not where he is.

7.   And what like of man was thy disciple?

8.   It was a boy who came to me in place of him who died, on account of the merit which I had gained when I bowed before the Law within there.

We read the following dialog in *Perelandra* by C. S. Lewis:

9.   But do I see you as you really are? he asked.

10.   Only Maledil sees any creature as it really is, said Mars.

11.   How do you see one another? asked Ransom.

12.   There are no holding places in your mind for an answer to that.

This dialog comes from Madeleine L'Engle's *A Wrinkle in Time*:

13.   The smallest beast, the one holding Meg, said, And perhaps they aren't used to visitors from other planets.

14.   Used to it! Calvin exclaimed, We've never had any, as far as I know.

15.   Why?

    I don't know.

16.   The middle beast, a tremor of trepidation in his words, said, You aren't from a dark planet, are you?   *(More practice for his lesson on next page.)

For 17-29, enclose titles of short literary works in quotation marks.

17. Oliver Wendell Holmes's poem, Old Ironsides, talks about a warship used in the War of 1812.

18. In his sermon entitled Selfishness, Charles Finney discusses this disease and gives a cure for it.

19. The class laughed heartily at Artemus Ward's two humorous essays, My Life Story and A Business Letter.

20. In Nathaniel Hawthorne's short story, The Great Carbuncle, eight people with varying motives all seek the precious jewel, but it is a risky business.

21. In the computer magazine, Robert read an interesting article, How to Create Your Own Website.

22. Today, the *Mud Valley News* published an editorial titled Educational Experimentation using Guinea Pigs.

23. Edgar Allen Poe's poem titled Alone describes how the author differs from other people.

24. Mr. Hake, a mathematician, gave a lecture entitled The Pythagorean Theorem for Dummies.

25. Washington Irving's article, A Republic of Prairie Dogs, attributes human qualities and characteristics to these little animals.

26. For his science class, Andrew wrote an essay called The Undefinable Black Hole.

27. Benito's short story, Life on the Princeton Levee, gained notoriety on the East Coast.

28. William Shakespeare wrote many longer plays, but he also wrote some short poems such as Under the Greenwood Tree.

29. Francis Bacon (1561-1626), an English philosopher, scientist, and writer, wrote an essay called On Revenge.

More Practice Lesson 69

Underline all words that should be italicized in print.

1. Shall we watch the movie Gone with the Wind, or would you rather see Mary Poppins?

2. "The Dance of the Sugar Plum Fairies" is a song from The Nutcracker.

3. The Zamora Family enjoyed the Phantom of the Opera.

4. Kurt plays and replays his CD entitled Veggie Tunes II.

5. Have you read that enchanting novel, The Hobbit, by J.R.R. Tolkien?

6. The aircraft carrier Enterprise entered the Persian Gulf.

7. We cruised Glacier Bay in Alaska on a ship called The Scandinavian Princess.

8. They saw Mona Lisa, Leonardo da Vinci's famous painting, when they visited the Louvre in Paris.

9. Leonardo da Vinci also painted Lady with an Ermine, which can be seen at the Czartoryski Museum in Cracow, Poland.

10. Years ago, we rode the train, Super Chief, from Los Angeles to Chicago.

11. The university owns a reproduction of Rodin's famous statue, The Thinker.

12. The Statue of Liberty welcomes immigrants to a land of opportunity.

13. In Melville's novel, Moby Dick, the evil Captain Ahab believes that he alone can conquer the white whale.

14. Aunt Isabel reads the Los Angeles Times newspaper every morning.

15. Uncle Gerardo subscribes to a magazine called Country Living.

Complete this irregular verb chart by writing the past and past participle forms of each verb.

	VERB	PAST	PAST PARTICIPLE
1.	beat		
2.	bite		
3.	bring		
4.	build		
5.	burst		
6.	buy		
7.	catch		
8.	come		
9.	cost		
10.	dive		
11.	drag		
12.	draw		
13.	drown		
14.	drive		
15.	eat		
16.	fall		
17.	feel		
18.	fight		
19.	flee		
20.	flow		
21.	fly		
22.	forsake		

Underline the correct verb form for each sentence.

1. Last night, Scot (beated, beat) Debby in chess.

2. Scot has (beat, beaten) Debby in every game this week.

3. Lydia (brang, brought) us some avocados from her tree.

4. She has (brung, brought) us avocados every year.

5. Last summer, Ed (builded, built) a new garage.

6. He has also (builded, built) a house for his dog.

7. Jim (buyed, bought) Nancy lunch.

8. He has (buyed, bought) her lunch several times this week.

9. During the first inning, Gaby (catched, caught) a high, fly ball in right field.

10. By the fourth inning, she had (catched, caught) seven fly balls.

11. Kim (comed, came) into the restaurant.

12. She said she had (came, come) to meet a friend.

13. Last Monday, bananas (costed, cost) 43¢ a pound.

14. They have (cost, costed) even more in the past.

15. Madeline (dove, dived) with perfect form!

16. She has never (dove, dived) with perfect form before.

17. Fernando (drawed, drew) the numbers from a hat.

18. He has not yet (drew, drawn) my number.

19. Yin (drived, drove) her parrot to the veterinarian.

20. The noisy parrot has nearly (drove, driven) Yin crazy.

21. Two feet of snow (falled, fell) yesterday.

22. How much snow has (falled, fell, fallen) this winter?

23. The crows and parrots (fighted, fought) over the walnuts.

24. They have (fighted, fought) over these nuts for years.

25. The helicopter (flew, flied) into a cloud.

26. Have you ever (flew, flown) in a helicopter?

Complete this irregular verb chart by writing the past and past participle forms of each verb.

VERB	PAST	PAST PARTICIPLE
1. give	_____	_____
2. go	_____	_____
3. hang (execute)	_____	_____
4. hang (dangle)	_____	_____
5. hide	_____	_____
6. hold	_____	_____
7. lay	_____	_____
8. lead	_____	_____
9. lend	_____	_____
10. lie (recline)	_____	_____
11. lie (deceive)	_____	_____
12. lose	_____	_____
13. make	_____	_____
14. mistake	_____	_____
15. put	_____	_____
16. raise	_____	_____
17. ride	_____	_____
18. rise	_____	_____
19. run	_____	_____
20. see	_____	_____
21. sell	_____	_____

Underline the correct verb form for each sentence.

1. Trini (given, gave) Juan her word.

2. She has (given, gave) him no reason to doubt her.

3. Effie (gone, went) to Greece last summer.

4. Has she (gone, went) every summer?

5. We (hanged, hung) a picture of George Washington in the library.

6. We have (hanged, hung) six pictures in all.

7. Edgar (hided, hid) his brother's birthday gift.

8. Perhaps he has (hid, hidden) it too well.

9. Fong gently (holded, held) the injured sparrow.

10. He has (held, holded) the sparrow all morning.

11. Olga (layed, laid) her recipe too close to the stove.

12. She should not have (laid, lain) the recipe there!

13. After lunch, exhausted construction workers (laid, lay) in the shade.

14. They have (laid, lain) there every day after lunch.

15. Unfortunately, Christie (losed, lost) her keys again.

16. Have you (losed, lost) yours also?

17. Adelina (maked, made) two hundred tamales.

18. She thought she had (maked, made) too many.

19. Last year, I (put, putted) my earnings in the bank.

20. I have (put, putted) four hundred dollars in the bank.

21. People (rised, rose) from their seats as the bride entered.

22. Mia had always (rose, risen) before dawn.

23. We (saw, seen) each other yesterday.

24. We have (saw, seen) each other every day.

25. Sheung (selled, sold) me his old bicycle.

Complete this irregular verb chart by writing the past and past participle forms of each verb.

	VERB	PAST	PAST PARTICIPLE
1.	set	_____	_____
2.	shake	_____	_____
3.	shine (light)	_____	_____
4.	shine (polish)	_____	_____
5.	shut	_____	_____
6.	sit	_____	_____
7.	slay	_____	_____
8.	sleep	_____	_____
9.	spring	_____	_____
10.	stand	_____	_____
11.	strive	_____	_____
12.	swim	_____	_____
13.	swing	_____	_____
14.	take	_____	_____
15.	teach	_____	_____
16.	tell	_____	_____
17.	think	_____	_____
18.	wake	_____	_____
19.	weave	_____	_____
20.	wring	_____	_____
21.	write	_____	_____

Underline the correct verb form for each sentence.

1. Yesterday, I (setted, set) my keys on this shelf.

2. I have always (setted, set) them there.

3. Baby Ben gurgled and (shook, shaked, shaken) his rattle.

4. He had never (shook, shaked, shaken) a rattle before.

5. Venus (shined, shone) brightly last night.

6. Sometimes, it has (shined, shone) even brighter.

7. Ms. Floosie (shined, shone) her black shoes before work.

8. She had (shined, shone) her shoes every Monday.

9. Effie (shutted, shut) her gate to keep the dog in the yard.

10. Have you (shutted, shut) your gate?

11. Rex the Gecko (sitten, sat) under the heat lamp.

12. Has he (sitted, sat) there for long?

13. Gloria (slept, sleeped) through the noisy commotion.

14. She must have (slept, sleeped) for twelve hours!

15. We (standed, stood) in line to buy tickets.

16. Have you ever (standed, stood) in that line?

17. Yesterday, James (swam, swum) for exercise.

18. He must have (swam, swum) two miles.

19. Has Debby (took, taken) Pantaloons to the dog groomer?

20. Yes, she (took, taken) Pantaloons to the groomer earlier.

21. Alba (teached, taught) me some Spanish vocabulary.

22. She had already (teached, taught) me the basics.

23. Has Ilbea (telled, told) you her funny story?

24. Yes, she (telled, told) us last night.

25. Have you (thinked, thought) about learning to cook?

26. Yes, I (thinked, thought) I would ask you to help me.

Hysterical Fiction #4

The Presidential Inauguration

Follows Lesson 73

Only one poet would be chosen to read his or her poem at the Presidential Inauguration on January 20. Many (1)_____ poets had entered the contest. Among
descriptive adjective

them was (2)_____, who had written a
proper noun (person)

(3)_____ poem about (4)_____.
descriptive adjective   abstract singular noun

(5)_____'s poem about (6)_____ was
proper noun (person)   concrete plural noun

(7)_____. It included (8)_____
comparative adjective   descriptive adjective

descriptions of (9)_____ that were
concrete plural noun

(10)_____   (11)_____
pres. participle form of verb   preposition

(12)_____.
concrete plural noun

Having spent (13)_____ (14)_____
number adjective   descriptive adjective

hours on a poem, (15)_____ entered the
proper noun (person)

(16)_____ poem of all. In this poem, a(n)
superlative adjective

(17)_____ tries (18)_____ and
concrete singular noun   infinitive form of verb

(19)_____   (20)_____
infinitive form of verb (transitive)   descriptive adjective

(21)_____   (22)_____
concrete plural noun   preposition

(23)_____.
abstract singular noun

The poet selected to read at the President's Inauguration

ceremony was (24)_____ with a poem entitled
proper noun (person)

(25)_____ about (26)_____ that apply to
feminine singular noun   abstract plural noun

all people. Future generations will read and perhaps enjoy

this (27)_____ poem.
descriptive adjective

Underline each adverb in these sentences.

1. Later, I clearly understood what had happened earlier.

2. Geese were honking very loudly, so I went out to shoo them away.

3. I had not quite succeeded when my neighbor Jean walked by.

4. Rather sourly, Jean scowled and told me that the geese should not leave.

5. "The geese were here first," she said defensively.

6. Completely annoyed, I shooed more vehemently and hollered stridently.

7. I jumped up and down and resolutely ignored my extremely rude neighbor.

8. I picked up acorns and tossed them everywhere, but the geese hardly noticed.

9. Soon, another gaggle of geese flew over and then landed nearby.

10. They stood still and studied me carefully as I continued to frantically jump and holler.

11. Entirely surrounded by honking geese, I barely noticed that Jean was throwing things too.

12. I wouldn't allow the geese to stay there.

13. I was too angry.

14. Meanwhile, Jean was casually tossing bread crumbs around.

15. More geese came even closer, and soon I couldn't move.

16. Bread crumbs sailed above, and the geese knocked me down.

17. Unable to stand up, I whimpered helplessly.

18. Geese honked above; I lay beneath; they had decidedly won.

Replace commas with semicolons where they are needed in these sentences.

1. U. S. cities with Spanish names include Los Angeles, California, Santa Fe, New Mexico, Pueblo, Colorado, and Amarillo, Texas.

2. Which interstate highway passes through Albuquerque, New Mexico, Amarillo, Texas, and Memphis, Tennessee?

3. Cecilia plays the bass guitar, Nedra plays the xylophone, drums, and cymbals.

4. Asparagus and turnips are vegetables, mangos, guavas, and tangelos are fruits.

5. Cecil washed his father's car today, moreover, he will wax it tomorrow.

6. Jenny ran five miles, biked ten miles, and swam two miles, consequently, she didn't want to play tennis with me.

7. I have painted houses, garages, and fences, however, I've never painted a car.

8. In October, a pound of apples cost 39¢, in November, 49¢, in December, 59¢, and in January, 99¢.

9. We painted all day, therefore, we finished before our guests arrived.

10. Monty and Allison will be here, also, Jenny will come if she can.

11. Ida creates beautiful sculptures, for example, she made an elephant and a giraffe last week.

12. Rob cleaned up the science lab, furthermore, he organized all the specimens and chemicals in the closet.

13. It was raining, nevertheless, I walked around the park for fresh air and exercise.

14. I forgot my umbrella, as a result, my clothes were soaking wet.

15. Would you rather explore Boston, Massachusetts, Cairo, Egypt, Madrid, Spain, or Copenhagen, Denmark?

Hysterical Fiction #5

A Fund Raising Event

Follows Lesson 90

The Federal election was only (1)_____
number adjective
months away. The (2)_____ Party, headed up by
descriptive adjective
(3)_____, was ready to begin raising funds for their
proper noun (person)
presidential candidate, (4)_____.
proper noun (person)
(5)_____, the party members would
adverb that tells "when"
(6)_____ cook a spaghetti dinner to be served in
adverb that tells "how"
(7)_____'s (8)_____ mansion in
proper noun (person)   descriptive adjective
(9)_____. The party members would search
proper noun (place)
(10)_____ and (11)_____ for wealthy,
adverb that tells "where"   adverb that tells "where"
(12)_____ who'd be willing to pay five hundred
descriptive adjective
dollars a plate for the (13)_____ of their lives.
superlative adjective

When the banquet day arrived, it became obvious that the
party members were better at (14)_____ and
pres. parrticiple form of verb
(15)_____ than cooking. They (16)_____
pres. participle form of verb   past tense of intransitive verb
as the sauce burned, and they (17)_____
past tense of transitive verb
(18)_____ as the noodles boiled over on the stove.
concrete plural noun

They proved (19)_____ cooks than the
comparative adjective
Democrats or the Repoblicans. (20)_____, they
adverb that tells "how"
earned enough money to pay (21)_____ to clean up
proper noun (person)
the mess in the kitchen. Perhaps next time they will serve
(22)_____ salmon and offer (23)_____,
descriptive adjective   pres. participle form of verb
(24)_____, or (25)_____ for
pres. participle form of verb   pres. participle form of verb
entertainment.

More Practice

Lesson 91

Use proofreading symbols to indicate corrections in the following writing samples.

1. We the People of the united States, in order to form a More perfect union, establish justice, insure domestic tranquility, provide for the common defense, promote the welfare general, and secure the blessings of liberty to ourselves and our posterity, do ordain and establish this Constitution for the United States America.

2. Ms. Tseng asked her class to write the U. S. Presidents in order. Sybils list began like this George Washington, Chester A. Arthur, John Adams, Thomas Jefferson, James Madison, James Monroe....

   Thats incorrect," said Ms. Tseng. "What's wrong with it?" asked Sybil. "Chester A. Arthur is the twenty first President, not the second," replied Ms. Tseng.

3. Congressional chaplains, the the official clergymen of Congress, oppen daily sessions of the House and Senate with prayer. This practice began with the Continental Congress in 1774 adn has continued ever since In 1789, the Senate elected Samuel Provoost, and the House elected the Reverend William Lynn as their first chaplains.

4. Article 2, Section 1 of the Constitution created the electoral college, the formalbody that elects the President of the United States Each state has as many electors in the electoral college as it has senators and representatives in Congress. On a date fixed by Congress, the people in each state vote for members of the electoral college. When citizens Vote for a President, they are actually voting for electors pledged to vote for their candidate. After the popular voting, the winning electors meet in there respective state capitals to cast one ballots for President and one ballot for Vice President.

More Practice Lesson 96

Insert apostrophes where they are needed in these sentences.

1. He couldnt remember where hed spent the Christmas of 93.

2. I dont recall his phone number, but Im sure it has several *4*s in it.

3. Theyre making Valentines and drawing *x*s and *o*s to represent kisses and hugs.

4. "Ive been standin in this line for an hour," he complained.

5. "Im sorry," said the cashier, "but weve been working as fast as we can."

6. Arent you curious about the meaning of her delphic comments?

7. Wasnt she born in 52?

8. You shouldnt say such bad things about the mayor; thats slander.

9. Hes ambivalent; he cant decide.

10. It wont last long, for its ephemeral.

11. Tomorrow, shell explain her primal objectives.

12. Id appreciate it if youd explain the meaning of the word *supine.*

13. The detective couldnt figure out the modus operandi of the thief.

14. In the past, theyve engaged in heated, ad hominem debates.

15. Weve photographed some herbivorous animals, but we havent seen any carnivorous animals yet.

16. Theres lightning lightening the sky, but there isnt any rain.

17. If youve driven that tortuous road, then youre aware of the twists and turns.

18. "Whats that honkin noise?" asked Milly.

19. "Jills practicin the trumpet," replied Bill.

20. I dont think its primal, but Im sure its important.

For 1–4, complete each sentence diagram.

1. Ancient Greeks admired physical fitness; citizens exercised at the public gymnasium.

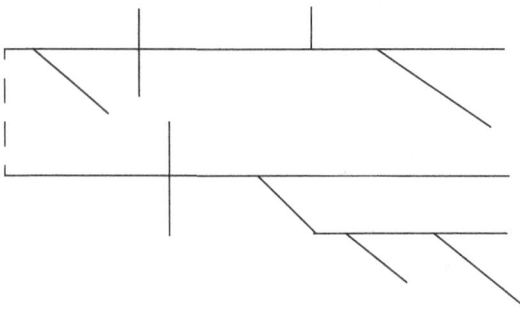

2. Asclepius, who usually carried a snake coiled around his staff, was the Greek god of healing.

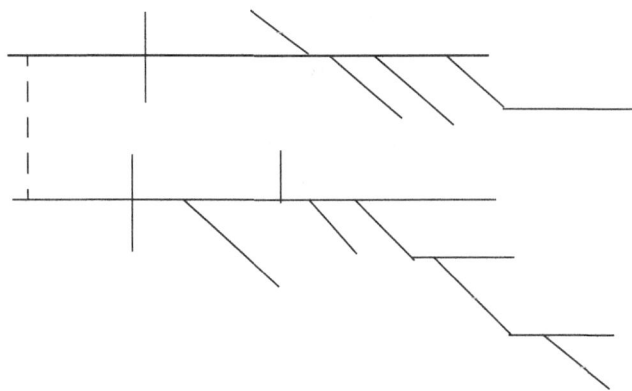

3. Hippocrates carefully observed patients' symptoms before he made a diagnosis.

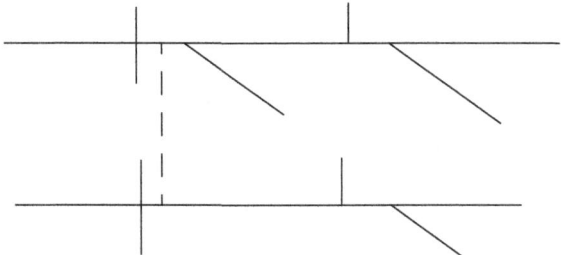

4. Having sworn the Hippocratic oath, Dr. Ngo gave his patients his best effort.

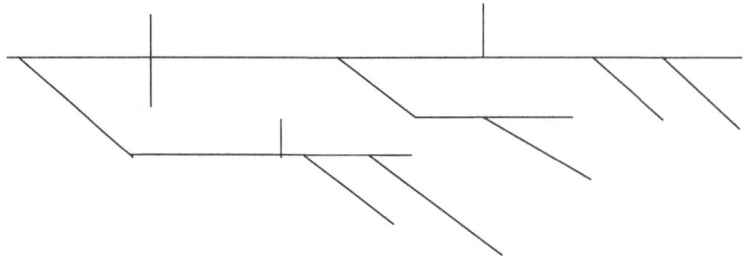

For 5–8, diagram each sentence in the space provided.

5. Developing more successful methods of healing was Hippocrates' goal.

6. Hippocrates, the founder of scientific medicine, practiced and taught on the island of Cos.

7. After we study the whole system, we can understand the various parts of the body.

8. The great Pericles died in a plague since the ancient world had no protection against epidemic diseases.

For fun, rewrite the following poem with correct spelling:

Spell Czech

Eye halve a spelling chequer. It came with my pea sea.

It plainly marques four my revue miss steaks eye kin knot sea.

Eye strike a key and type a word and weight four it two say

Weather eye am wrong oar write. It shows me strait a weigh.

As soon as a mist ache is maid, it nose bee fore two long,

And I can put the error rite. Its rarely ever wrong.

Eye have run this poem threw it, I am shore your pleased two no.

Its letter perfect in its weigh. My chequer tolled me sew.

—Sauce Unknown